LIFE AT HAMILTON

LIFE AT HAMILTON

Sometimes You Throw Away Your Shot, Only To Find Your Story

MIKE ANTHONY

Printed in the United States of America

First Printing, 2021

ISBN-13: 978-1-947637-57-3 print edition
ISBN-13: 978-1-947637-58-0 ebook edition

Waterside Productions
2055 Oxford Ave
Cardiff, CA 92007
www.waterside.com

To Mom. I may have written the words, but you made them.

And to Victoria, Jake, Olivia and Sage.
It's good to know you are the ones coming to save the world.

ACKNOWLEDGMENTS

You know what's way better than writing a book?

Getting stuck writing a book.

So then, one morning, your whole family, like, all of them, sit around on a Zoom call with you for two hours, as they try to help.

Know what's better than that? Going to your sister's house to drop the book off so she can read it when she has time, but instead, she doesn't let you leave until seven hours later—literally seven hours later—after she has read the entire thing, out loud, and we've pinpointed what we think some issues are.

I'll tell you what—I'm so excited to be publishing this. It's something little me never imagined, way back there, trying to envision what it would all be. But someday, when I'm ready to slip to another dimension, I'm not going to think about the book. I'm going to think about those faces looking back at me from the screen on the Zoom call. I'm going to think of my sister's hoarse voice, coming from a still smiling face, and those of my brother-in-law and niece and nephew when I finally left their house in the middle of the night.

Writing a book is great. But it'll never compare to those faces.

The most important gift I've been given is my tendency to look for the good stuff. And the reason for that tendency is simple; I grew up with the good stuff. This book was written because Elizabeth Bonaldo is my mom, Robert Anthony is my dad, and Jennifer D'Amato and Stefanie D'Amato are my sisters. I gravitate towards what's right with the world, because these people are my world. Thanks to Gordon, Toma, Donna, Anthony, Reco, my nieces and nephew, Aunt Carol and Uncle Jim, Jamie, Uncle Roger and Aunt Roseanne, Sheri, Roger, indeed, my whole family, for this book.

Nick Marcotti. Thanks to you, my friend. Because of you, I laugh the same way now as I did when I was a kid, with the same abandon, and just as often. So, this book is because of you, too. And because of Amie and Amy and Andrew and Andrew and Marie and Andy and Tamara and Sara and Sarah and the other Nick, and Katie and Kat and Gabe and Jessie and Julia and Heather and Anna and AnnMarie and Nicole and Alex and Rich and Chip and Mike, and all those friends I've grown up with (no matter how little growing I actually did) and every friend I've made along the way. This book would not have happened without having met you. I truly wish there was space here to mention every name, with a description of what you've individually meant to me and taught me. But that would be a book unto itself.

And to those I "work" with every day. I love what we do because of you. Marie Toruño and Andy Phelan especially—you have blessed my life. Thank you, Andy, Christine Penski, and Bill Youmans for the insightful feedback, and Tim Pettolina, thanks for all you've done to help make this happen, and for making it all a joy.

Thanks to Ramesh Ganershram, and others like him, who early on pushed me in this direction. Your pushing made this book.

Thanks to Leslie Kean, who, when she isn't changing the world with her reporting in the New York Times about UFOs or writing paradigm-shifting books exploring evidence for what might come after this life, somehow finds time to read an early draft of her friend's book, and provide guidance and insight to mold the unwieldy mess into something a person who didn't birth me might want to read.

Thank you Jennifer Houle. The way a book feels is so much more than the words inside. I think I've always known that, subconsciously, but Jen's work designing both the cover and the interior of *Life At Hamilton* has brought it to the front and center of my attention. She's made the book the best home these words could have.

And R. Stephanie Good. Without her selfless, unending assistance, this book would not have been made a reality. Through countless hours, she found every extra comma and misplaced clause. And here is the part I'm certain is most rare;

knowing actor/bartender/mostly bartenders often aren't deep in extra money, she copy-edited this book entirely out of the kindness of her heart, and nothing more. All of that work for a "thank you." And even that I had to urge her to let me print.

And Lin. Without the shows you've given us, and the familial atmosphere you create when producing them, this book surely would not have come to be. To know you've read the following words is an honor. (And nuts).

And finally, to all of the virtual friends I've made along this journey. Without you, certainly, this book would have remained another of the infinite potentials waiting to manifest. Your support brought it into existence.

So, you see, the book you are about to read doesn't belong to me. I hope you enjoy what we've done.

CONTENTS

LIFE AT HAMILTON

ACT 1, SCENE 1

LIGHTS UP

"Oh, the places you'll go!"

—DR. SEUSS

I couldn't believe it.

I'd made it.

I was here . . . Broadway.

As thirteen-hundred people wildly rose to their feet in thunderous applause, a single tear, exquisitely summoned by my seven years and $100,000 worth of actor training, slipped down my cheek and splashed upon the stage as I took my bow. I'd just delivered the performance of a lifetime, lifetimes even, and the audience was doing what they could to thank me, with the little energy they had left, having been wrung dry of every emotion by my acting. As they clapped and cried, knowing they'd just witnessed something the likes of which they'd not before, and shan't again, I humbly motioned for the rest of the cast, applauding for me themselves, they too, wet with tears, to join me at the front of the stage. I wanted to let them know I could not have given the performance I did without them (though, I mean, I probably could have) and wanted them to take a bow (a quick one) for themselves, and they did, but then again pushed me out from the line to stand, once more, alone at the front of the stage, flowers now raining down upon me. This was everything I'd always dreamed it would be, and then some. The thought of my mom saying to me, many years ago, that if ever I became famous, she knew it wouldn't change me one bit, flashed in my mind, and I wondered if she was right. To remain humble after this would certainly be a challenge, but I resolved, for her, to try. And then, just as I put my hand to my heart in deep thanks, one voice from within the cacophony of praise rose from the din and pierced my ears. "Hey!" it shouted. Then "HEY!" again, even louder, as the theater suddenly emptied. I was now looking at thirteen-hundred empty seats, the scene before me dissolved instantly by the voice, every rose disappearing before my eyes as I heard it once more,

"YO! Get off the stage!"

I looked to my left to find the bearded face of a security person, with not quite enough beard to hide its wearer's disdain.

"Oh . . . sorry," I said with a smile. "I didn't see you there. It's okay, I work here," I proudly told him. "It's my first day. I'm a bartender!"

"That's awesome. Get off the stage."

And so began my Broadway career.

★

I had recently moved back to New York City after receiving my MFA in acting, and with my combined $100,000 educational debt had gotten a job working for a concessions company that serviced the eight Nederlander theaters on Broadway. It could not have been more thrilling to walk through the stage door of the Richard Rodgers that day if I were in the show itself—a new musical I knew nothing about called *In the Heights*. Just to be in a theater where so much magic had happened over its hundred-year history, even simply as a bartender, felt profound. The security guy didn't quite see it that way, it seemed, as he ushered me off the stage and into the lobby.

The lobby, it was made clear, was my domain. I was not allowed on the stage.

The following day was to be the first preview for *In the Heights*, the first time an audience would see the show. The Rodgers had been closed for a month as the set from *Cyreno de Bergerac* was moved out and *In the Heights* moved in, and the intervening days had gathered some dust. I was there, therefore, to get things cleaned up and ready for service.

As I worked behind a bar on the orchestra level, a man came up to me and asked, "Hey man, do you have any of those show cups?"

Each show had recently started selling their drinks in souvenir cups with the show's logo on them. This was the first I'd seen of this man, but figured he was probably an usher or merchandise seller.

"No," I said. "They haven't been printed yet. But we should have them by opening night. Are you . . . do you work here?"

"I'm with the show, yeah."

"Oh okay, cool. If you come back after opening, we can get you them."

"Great. Thanks!"

And he walked away.

The next afternoon I took a break from cleaning liquor pourers and ice scoops and slipped into the theater to watch some of the rehearsal that was going on. People were milling about on stage as the technical team worked something out, when I caught sight of him. *Oh look,* I said to myself with some surprise, *it's the cup guy.* The man who'd asked for the cups was on stage. I recalled my first time on that stage the day before and thought, *Watch out, Cup Guy. Beard Guy doesn't mess around.* Someone from out in the darkness of the house said into a microphone, "From the top!" Everyone exited, and the theater went dark. Lone drumsticks beat out a rhythm and the lights suddenly came up.

On the cup guy.

Cup Guy was standing center stage, and no one tackled him. As it turned out, he wasn't just *with* the show, he was *in* the show, and kicked it off as he started telling this story in a mesmerizing rapping style.

I took a Playbill from atop a stack sitting on the steps, ready to hand to audience members when the show had its first public performance later that evening, and flipped to the section with the acting company's headshots and biographies. There I found that the cup guy was Lin-Manuel Miranda, who played Usnavi, one of the central characters in the piece. Upon further inspection, I realized that Mr. Miranda had his name in quite a few places in the Playbill, having conceived *In the Heights,* and written the music and lyrics, as well.

Cup Guy wasn't just *in* the show. He *was* the show.

That night, at the end of the first preview performance, I watched Lin live out the fantasy I'd had when standing right on the spot where he now stood, with thirteen-hundred real people, louder even than the figments of my imagination, utterly losing their minds as the final note was struck.

This show—this man—it was clear, was something special.

For the first two weeks, I watched the show every spare second I could in between serving drinks to patrons. I was completely transfixed. Lin had seamlessly thread together multiple styles into one perfect piece. The music and the choreography and his spitfire lyrics kept me at the theater each night far later than I needed to be—bartenders can leave after intermission, but I stayed every night to watch until the end.

A few weeks later, Lin returned to the bar, again seeking the cups with his show's logo on them.

"Hey," he said, coming up to me one night before we opened the house. "Do you know who I talk to about getting a bunch of those souvenir cups?"

"Yes. That's me. I'm Mike—we met a few weeks ago."

"Oh, right!"

Knowing the writer and star of a show is often keen to get opinions from the bartender, I said, "Listen. I've got some notes. Not many. Mostly, things look good. But why don't we think about losing the rap stuff?" He broke into a grin as I continued, "To be serious, you're a genius. I mean, I think you might be like, you know, like an actual genius."

I don't recall this conversation verbatim, but I do remember thinking, as soon as Lin walked away, *Dude* (which, I guess, is what I call myself to myself after being disappointed with myself), *you can't say 'like' that much when you're talking to a genius! I mean really, you should always try to limit that, but especially when conversing with a genius. And most especially a linguistic genius. Like, come on!*

I meant it, though—I felt, on the very first night of the show, that I was in the presence of someone with an exquisite ability—something akin in scope and singularity to Mozart or Da Vinci. And one evening, when the sound system went down right before the show was set to begin, those suspicions about Lin's brain being a once-in-a-generation sort of brain were confirmed. About fifteen minutes past what was supposed to be curtain time, the large audience was getting restless. An announcement was made that they were experiencing technical difficulties (which is not entirely uncommon for a Broadway musical as it works out the kinks during the month-long preview period) and soon after that, Lin walked out onto the stage. The audience got quiet as he introduced himself (which was necessary at that time—I doubt Lin will ever need to introduce himself again). He then began speaking with a person in the audience, asking their name, where they were from, what they'd done that day, etc. He did that with about four more people, making typical small talk. But then something extraordinary happened; he began to do a monologue about all of those people, in the rapid, rhythmic style we'd grown accustomed to hearing in *In The Heights*—a show that took years to write and perfect. But here Lin was, writing a story in that style on the spot. He went on to do a ten-minute improvised rap about those people, using all of the information he'd just gathered. It was stunning. Somehow, in the moment he was saying one thing, one funny and creative thing, another part of him was figuring out the next—and making it all rhyme. In fifteen minutes, he met people, learned a bit about them, and then simultaneously wrote and performed a rhyming verse play. Folks, I worked on this paragraph for five hours. And after just this one rhyme, I need a shower. (Does "hours" and "shower" even rhyme?)

As it turned out, the technical issue regarding the sound system proved to be a bigger problem than they could solve that evening, so the show never went on. But standing behind the bar, listening to people as they exited, I sensed a thrill in the air. You might expect those in attendance to be quite annoyed that the evening they'd planned had a wrench thrown into it, and having to now go through the hassle of getting their tickets exchanged for another performance, but on the contrary, most seemed to feel they'd just experienced something one-of-a-kind, something they'd always remember. They didn't get to see the show, but my, did they have a story to tell.

Most of us in the house that night were wholly unaware, at that time, of Freestyle Love Supreme, which is an improvisational hip-hop group Lin started while at Wesleyan University, performing on sidewalks. It's sidewalks no more, though, as the group has since had its own highly acclaimed run on Broadway. Those in the audience that night were getting just a taste of things to come from that once-in-a-generation brain/heart combo.

When the official opening night finally arrived and the first act went on, my instincts about how remarkably good the show was were confirmed by round after round of sustained applause wafting out from the theater. I smiled and rested my head in my hands and, with the mellifluous poetry and cadence of Lin's soon-to-be-hit soundtracking my imaginings, dreamed, there in the lobby, about the day coming soon when I'd not be in the lobby, but instead, in the room so nearby where magic was happening. With my new MFA in hand, and this great new job where I would be so close to wonderful people happy to help my career, it was easy to believe Vanessa, a character in the show who longed for better things ahead, as her words floated so hopefully into my ears; "It won't be long now . . . any day."

And then ten years passed.

Just like that.

As shows opened and closed, and unknown actors made their debuts and later found fame and fortune, and coworkers came and went when their own careers took off, there, behind the bar, was me.

WE KEEP MEETING

"Men give me credit for some genius. All the genius I have lies in this; when I have a subject in hand, I study it profoundly. Day and night it is before me. My mind becomes pervaded with it. Then the effort that I have made is what people are pleased to call the fruit of genius. It is the fruit of labor and thought."

—ALEXANDER HAMILTON

"How'd you do it, Lin? How did you get through that?"

One very late evening not long after *In the Heights* had closed, while bowling for the Broadway Show League, I asked Lin that question, wondering from what bottomless well he could have pulled the focus to maintain composure during the final performance.

"It's the hardest thing I've ever done," he said.

When the producers decided that the show's three year run would soon be coming to an end, Lin, along with several other members of the original cast, chose to return for the final months. I, of course, had been there all along, and though I'd never intended to be bartending for that long, when the notice of the closing came down, I wasn't ready for it to end.

Working at *In the Heights* was a truly transformative experience. What my high school director told us about theater being "a tool to change the world" was no longer just a nice concept—for three years I watched the reality that the right words and voices and movements put together in the right ways can reach peoples' hearts, and alter who they are. This was made clear by the dedicated fan base that had grown around the show. People would often come over and over again, reveling in the gift of *In the Heights*, and the fact that live theater is a new experience each time, no matter how often a show's score is found to be inadvertently hummed, or how easily it's lyrics fall trippingly off the tongue.

But never was the full impact of Lin's first Broadway show more apparent than on closing night, when the depth of its affect was brought roaring home, and about which I couldn't help but ask Lin before he sent a gutter ball down the alley (does it help to know that no one is good at everything?).

When he made his final first entrance on January 9th, 2011, the audience went so wild he had to pause as he looked upstage, trying perhaps, to reign in his emotions. The crowd eventually quieted enough for him to begin, but that rousing display of appreciation would only be the first of many to come from the emotionally invested and extremely lively audience. In fact, the performance ran twenty minutes longer than usual that night, so extended were the applauses between (and often during) scenes. During the song "Blackout," in which the lights go out, leaving the theater in darkness, members of the cast open their cellphones to provide some illumination. On this night, Lin turned around to find nearly the entire audience had done the same. It was an overwhelmingly emotional experience, and it is difficult to understand how the cast continued to stay so focused as the crowd let loose. If it had been me turning around to see the joy I'd brought reflected back at me by all of those people shouting and laughing and crying—including members of the cast who were not in the show that night, and some who'd participated in the run at one time or another who'd returned to watch the final performance, who sat on the steps beside myself and most of the house staff, crying and singing loudly along—if I'd spun around to look out into that sea of love and gratitude, seeing in a moment how deeply so many had been touched by something I'd created, I'd have been reduced to a wet, snotty mess crumpled up on the stage floor, unable to eek out another word, let alone continue singing. But not Lin. He, and the entire cast, somehow transformed the energy into ever-greater focus, delivering performances forever etched in the memories of those in the room. When the curtain came down for the last time, Lin thanked everyone in his remarkable way, improvising a rapped wrap up before walking off the stage and leaving me grateful to have experienced such a thing, and sad that the lights would not come up on Washington Heights tomorrow. I couldn't help but wonder, though, on where they might shine next.

Now, if all you ever did with the whole of your life was put *In the Heights* into the world, you would have done quite enough. If we get but one shot at being a person, and the only thing you accomplished with it was to add this eruption of creativity and life to our story—you would have spent that opportunity well. You could feel okay sitting on a beach somewhere for the rest of time, sipping Pina

Coladas and enjoying the fact that you'd made a thing—a thing that would bring joy to untold numbers for many years to come. But as influential and musical-landscape-changing as his first show was, Lin, as it turned out, was quite far from done, with an even greater something lying within him, not so patiently waiting for its time to burst out from his heart, and into ours.

In the decade since *In the Heights* had taken Broadway by storm, while I'd worked my way up from bartender to manager of the bar (a feat which could easily happen in three months) Lin was working behind the scenes not on breaking the Pina Colada record, thankfully for us, but on his next creation. Having read a biography about our "ten dollar founding father," Lin's mind began to do its thing, which eventually resulted in a new show called *Hamilton: An American Musical.*

As *Hamilton* performed its off-Broadway run at The Public, whispers were making their way uptown that this was a masterpiece. Working on Broadway, you could not escape the buzz that was being generated. And when word came that Lin wanted to use his old stomping grounds for his new venture, the staff at The Richard Rodgers were ecstatic—"Have you heard? Did you hear? We might be getting *Hamilton!*" And when it was officially announced that it would, indeed, be making our theater its Broadway home, the place was electric.

The day before the show was to have its first preview, I was in the lobby, just as I was ten years earlier, readying for the public. Marie, my fellow bartender, and I were putting together drink menus specific to *Hamilton*, and adding new lights around the bar, when I heard footsteps approach and turned to see my good friend, the house manager for the Richard Rodgers, Tim Pettolina.

"They've invited you guys to watch the last run-through," he said.

Lin, being the inclusive sort that he is, wanted the house staff to have the unique opportunity of seeing the show, with just us, just the "HamFam," before it was to be released to the world on the following day.

"Sure," I said. "We'll be right in."

I hung up the last row of lights, and Marie and I made our way into the theater.

Truth be told, I didn't know much about Hamilton the man, and nothing at all about the show, other than that my old "pal" Lin had written it, and there was something of a "Beatlemania" aura already surrounding it. I knew that Hamilton had been a "founding father," thought he might have been a president, and was fairly sure he'd been involved in a duel with somebody (maybe John Quincy Adams? Or the other Adams, perhaps? Wasn't there another Adams?), that he'd either won, lost, or tied. So, when the lights went down that night, the night before the first Broadway preview, and Marie and I sat in the near empty theater, I had no real sense of what was about to happen. How the world—and, more immediately, *my* world—was about to change. I had no idea what to expect.

Well . . . that's not entirely true—I had *some* idea. For *Hamilton*, Lin had brought together the same creative team that had given us *In the Heights*, including Tommy Kail as director, Alex Lacamoire as the music director, and Andy Blankenbuehler as the choreographer. So, when we settled into our seats to behold, for the first time, their next collaboration, knowing the previous alchemical results of mixing the talents of these four together, it's inaccurate to say I had no idea of what was to come. I did. But that idea would not be big enough to contain what we experienced that evening—no matter which Adams Hamilton had killed.

Having the choice of any seat in the house, Marie and I picked the first row of the mezzanine. We sat beside another co-worker and a few of the swings and understudies. It was just us, thirteen-hundred empty seats, and *Hamilton*. A spotlight came up, and a character entered that I didn't yet know, but would intimately by the end of the evening, speaking directly to us in a syncopation that we fell immediately into, as our heads began to move with the beat. *I wish we could always talk like this*, I thought. A meaning not only in the words, but also within the rhythm in which they were spoken, began to penetrate my subconscious. More characters stepped onto the stage, some, I was delighted to find, being played by actors from *In the Heights'* original cast, each adding more and more context to the story in a tempo, at first steady and slow, but with a growing energy we sensed beneath, ready to explode at any second. It felt like I imagined it must as a kid watching space shuttle launches when the thrusters begin to burn, and there is a low rumble, and then a shake as the pressure builds. You feel the rumble in your body, in your bones, in all of you, and as anticipation of the release of the power grows within, you start to feel the moment coming when the restraints will let go, and it will hurtle into the sky. As the first number went on, that's what it felt like—as though we were atop a rocket, and in for the ride of our lives. And we were right. Throughout the evening, Lin masterfully released this energy, soaring to ever greater heights, and all we could do was try to hang on. By the end, Marie was sobbing beside me. She was actually rocking back and forth in her chair, unable to wrangle the feelings the show had elicited. When the final note rang out, the seven or so of us watching in that big empty house gave the wildest standing ovation we could muster, weak as we were from the rocket ride's expended emotion. *Hamilton* was everything we'd been hearing it was.

And much, much more.

I'd been worried the show may have been overhyped, but mere minutes in I felt such a thing is not possible. And two hours later, I knew everyone in the world had to experience it. Had I Lin's verbal dexterity, I might be able to properly express how and why the show evoked in us the visceral reactions that it did. Since there's only one LMM, I'll leave it at this: some things are simply ineffable, and must be experienced firsthand. No description of Niagara Falls comes close to being in that boat just beneath them.

Afterwards, Tommy Kail gave notes to the assembled cast seated in the orchestra. From a few rows away, I listened as he, like a coach addressing his team before the big game, thanked them for their hard work, their talent, and the beautiful thing they had accomplished together. There was a sense among the group, already, that something quite extraordinary was happening, that they had captured the proverbial lighting in a bottle, and Tommy tried to prepare them for the wild ride they were about to take, when they would finally, the next day, "Uncork this thing on the world."

And uncorked it was.

ACT 1, SCENE 3

HERE COMES THE GENERAL

"In the unlikely story that is America, there has never been anything false about hope. For when we have faced down impossible odds, when we've been told we're not ready or that we shouldn't try or that we can't, generations of Americans have responded with a simple creed that sums up the spirit of a people: Yes, we can. Yes, we can. Yes, we can."

—BARACK OBAMA

After that first preview, the already legendary status of a show that would not officially open for another month took on a near mythical air. The "word on the street" was that *Hamilton* was, perhaps, the best piece of theater, of any variety, to ever hit the stage anywhere in the whole of time and space. And if the hype hadn't already been bolstered to the heights of hyperbole, we were about to have a visitor that would propel the bourgeoning juggernaut even further into the stratosphere.

It's no secret that then President Barack Obama was a big fan of Lin's – so much so that when the White House decided to present "An Evening of Poetry, Music, and Spoken Word" in May 2009, he invited Lin to perform.

Not long before that presidential invitation, Lin, while on vacation during the run of *In the Heights*, read Ron Chernow's biography of Hamilton, and, as anyone would, imagined it might make a good hip hop concept album where different renowned rappers contribute songs to a mix tape, each playing different historical figures. (Who wouldn't have come to the very same conclusion?) One of these characters was Aaron Burr, for whom, by the time the White House called, Lin had written a song—the song that would eventually become the opening number of the *Hamilton* the world now knows. When Obama phoned, Lin figured it was the perfect time to debut the piece. Needless to say, the President and First Lady (and everyone else in the room) were blown away by the performance, and couldn't wait to see what would become of the project. So, it should not have come as a shock to me the day that Tim, the house manager, pulled me aside to say in an animated but hushed tone, "The President is coming tomorrow."

"The president? Of what?"

"Of . . . here . . . of us . . . of Amer . . . The President of the United States!"

But it *was* a shock, one that, in fact, left me weak in the knees.

See, up until my dad's passing in 2011, the worst day of my life had been September 11th of 2001. Around that time, I was temping on and off for a company in tower two of the World Trade Center. The days I worked always changed, so on that Tuesday morning, my mom didn't know whether or not I was in the building. As it turned out, I was off that day and in bed when she called. "Hi Mom," I sleepily said. And she immediately started to cry with what I would soon find out was relief.

"What's wrong?" I asked, with no small degree of worry. She told me what had happened, and I ran into the living room to turn on the television. My phone rang again, this time with my girlfriend, Heather, on the other end of the line.

"Have you heard?"

"Yes. What a terrible accident."

"I know," she said.

At that time, only the first plane had hit, and neither she, my mom, nor I ever imagined someone would try to do such a thing on purpose. Heather was working in the Chrysler building at the time and had a clear view of the towers from her office windows. She and her coworkers were all gathered, watching the awful scene unfold. I was sitting on my couch, flipping from channel to channel, all of which were now covering the story. Then, I heard a horrible scream over the phone. Heather and those she was with had just seen something my slightly delayed news channel hadn't yet broadcast until a split second later, when, as I was yelling into the phone, "What's the matter? Are you okay? What's wrong?" I saw on the screen playing over the anchor's shoulder, the second plane hit.

The following hours were an absolute and utter nightmare. In the chaos that unfolds at a time like that, many false stories and partial truths were being bandied about, including the possibility that there was some type of chemical or biological agent in the smoke from the buildings, or that other planes were still on their way to other targets. By the time the plane hit the Pentagon, we were in a full-blown this-feels-like-the-end-of-the-world panic.

Heather and I lived in Queens, and the subway system had been completely shut down, so she had to walk all the way from the Chrysler building and over the 59th Street Bridge to get home. When she finally did, she fell into my arms saying nothing, and cried.

Over the course of the following years, many tears would flow. For Heather and I, and so very many others, the fall of the towers was just the beginning of an extended trauma that continued and grew with the invasion of Afghanistan and then Iraq—wars of which we could not see the end. Maintaining optimism during George W. Bush's presidency was, for me, intensely difficult.

But then, from my perspective, a miracle happened.

And I was about to meet him.

------------ ★ ------------

July 18, 2015

As I removed my belt and emptied my pockets into a tray, a Secret Service agent asked if it would be okay to pat me down.

"Yes," I said. "I hear you guys are really, really good at the pat down. Like, maybe even the best!" To which the agent said nothing, offering no more than a steely-eyed glare.

And that's when I learned that the salient characteristic of the United States Secret Service is not a sense of humor.

After giving me a very thorough check, one that felt as though my checker should have been wearing a stethoscope and asking how often I exercise, I was allowed to enter the theater as a throng of people gathered around a closed-down 46th Street in Manhattan.

I couldn't quite believe it. In a matter of hours, I'd be in a room with Barack Obama.

I first became aware of Obama in 2004 when he gave the keynote speech at the Democratic National Convention. Like so many others, I eagerly asked, "Who is *that* guy? Why can't I vote for *him*?" When, four years later, he threw his hat into the presidential campaign ring, though the thought of him pulling off a long shot surprise filled me with elation, I didn't think we were, as a country, *there* yet.

Working in the arts, people who tend to be sensitive to cultural issues—Kurt Vonnegut's "canaries in the coal mine"—are my friends and coworkers, so the fact that racism in this country is alive and well is something of which I'm very much aware. Hearing people in my life, whose skin happens to be on the darker end of the human skin tone spectrum, describe what it is like to be them, to be in their bodies, where store clerks immediately become suspicious as soon as they enter, and whose hearts begin to pound if, goodness forbid, the flashing lights of a police cruiser should suddenly appear in their rearview mirrors, makes me cognizant of the frighteningly sad reality that we have not come as far as we sometimes think. (And of course, after the horrifying murder of George Floyd, these issues have bubbled again to the surface, this time with a force not seen in a long time, a force of such impact you don't need to be a canary to sense it).

So, when Obama announced his candidacy, as thrilled as I was, I didn't allow myself to get my hopes up, knowing they'd be dashed if I did.

But gosh, it was difficult to not get my hopes up. The words he spoke were an antidote to the despair I'd often felt over the previous eight years, and I found myself listening to them over and over. So inspiring was he that the Black Eyed Peas made a video using the speech he gave after losing the New Hampshire Primary, in which he'd said:

> It was a creed written into the founding documents that declared the destiny of a nation:
> Yes, we can.
> It was whispered by slaves and abolitionists as they blazed a trail towards freedom through the darkest of nights: Yes, we can.
> It was sung by immigrants as they struck out from distant shores and pioneers who pushed westward against an unforgiving wilderness: Yes, we can.
> It was the call of workers who organized, women who reached for the ballot, a president who chose the moon as our new frontier, and a king who took us to the mountaintop and pointed the way to the promised land:
> Yes, we can, to justice and equality.
> Yes, we can, to opportunity and prosperity.
> Yes, we can heal this nation.
> Yes, we can repair this world.
> Yes, we can.

As the tears came to my eyes with each speech he gave, I grieved at the not-yet-missed "missed" chance of having a poet as president. *How wonderful it will be*, I thought, *when the day mercifully arrives that a person like this, no matter their color or gender or anything superficial, can get elected to the Presidency of the United States, judged oh-so-finally on the content of their character. What a world it will be when a person like this is the leader of it.*

But I knew it wasn't to be. We just weren't there.

So, on election night, as I sat in my sister's living room with her and her family and our mom and stepfather and my girlfriend, all of us firmly in Barack Obama's corner, and the results started to role in, only then did I allow myself to believe it might actually happen. And when it did, when the election was officially called, there wasn't pandemonium and boisterous celebration in my sister's living room; there was silence. As my girlfriend, who was sitting beside me, squeezed me tightly, I looked through my teary eyes into hers, then around the room. No one spoke, I realized, because no one could. In our eyes, a miracle had just taken place, and the enormity of it overwhelmed our vocal cords. Instead, we just hugged and cried and marveled. And when Obama and his family walked oh so steadily out onto that historic stage in Chicago, so superhumanly shouldering this unfathomable burden, and the impossible hope of "Yes we can" turned into the concrete reality of "Yes we did," in the most sublime speech my ear bones had ever vibrated with, well, it was one of the happiest moments of my life. Even my dad, a lifelong fiscally-minded Republican, after our months upon months of family-gathering-debates, called me and said, "Congratulations. I think he'll do a good job."

Obama's election was, for me, like waking up from an eight-year nightmare to a beautiful, perfect, sunny summer day. It entirely changed the way I felt about the world, and my day-to-day personal happiness was affected—something no other election had precipitated.

So, when I was told, one day, out of the blue, that I needed to come in early the next to unlock my office and safe so the Secret Service could do a sweep because Barack Obama was coming to see *Hamilton*, as you might imagine, I was beside myself.

Which led to my unappreciated exuberance with the Secret Service.

Once in, I dropped my bag off in my office, which had been left unlocked and open, and I noticed that things had been moved around. When a president visits a place, the security apparatus that swings into motion is far bigger than I'd ever envisioned. Hundreds of people are involved—and those are just the ones in uniforms or suits wearing special pins and talking into their wrists. I imagined the snipers invisibly camped out on rooftops around the theater, and wondered how many more plain-clothed officers of various agencies were among us. The whole operation, the task of keeping a president safe in a big city, is almost unimaginably large.

As our staff slowly made their way through the security checks, with less attempted jokes than me, they trickled in. The lobby was swirling with Secret Service and people in other unrecognized uniforms as we worked to set up the bars. I wondered if one of them was carrying the briefcase of nuclear codes, or "football," as it's commonly known. At one point, a bartender dropped a bottle which made a loud sound, and for a moment I thought I might turn around to see her tackled to the floor. "It's just a bottle, it's just a bottle!" I said, putting my hands in the air—which solicited, for the first time, just the hint of a smile from one of the agents. Thinking I might have cracked his icy exterior, I walked up to him and quietly said, "What can you tell me about Roswell? Do we actually have alien bodies in a military base somewhere? I promise I won't tell anyone. Come on, I really, really promise. Really. Tell me? The secret will be safe. Do we?" To which, quite to my surprise, he said, with a full smile now, "Sorry, I can't discuss that. I mean I could, but I'd have to . . . well, you know the rest."

We got the bars set up, and at some point, it became clear something was afoot. The activity in the lobby increased, and I knew the moment I'd been waiting for since his speech in 2004 was upon me; within moments, the caravan of the President of the United States would pull up to the theater, and through the special tent entryway they'd set up, Barack Obama would appear.

As I walked with an empty ice bucket to the back alley where our ice machine is, an agent put up his hand, stopping me. "Can I help you?" he asked.

"I'm just getting ice for the bar," I answered.

"One minute," he said.

He then talked into his wrist (just like in the movies!), asking some sort of question. I imagined all sorts of high-tech hidden cameras suddenly trained on me—and maybe other things, too. It was intimidating, but gosh darn it, the bar needed ice, and I wasn't about to let the bar down. There would be no warm drinks. Not on this day. (Cue the heroic music, please).

The agent received an inaudible okay, and I was allowed to pass through the large door leading to the ice machine room in the back alley. Swinging it closed behind me and making sure it clicked into place as I every day did, trying somehow with the clicking into place to let everyone know that this was exactly how I clicked that door every single time I closed it, and today's clicking was no different, it mattered not who might be behind the door, somewhere, I didn't care, I am as unperturbed as I ever am, closing this door in the exact same way I always do. Maintaining what I knew was a James Bond level of calm and cool and collected, closing that door with such something that I felt the Secret Service might be thinking, *We should get this guy's resume—no one closes a door that stoically,* I looked up from the handle mechanism, and there he was.

Taller than I'd imagined (though, with my five-foot-six frame, most people are taller than I'd imagined), but with just as warm a smile, Barack Obama, the 44th President of the United States, stood in a makeshift waiting area.

"Oh my gosh," I said.

I know now what kinds of sounds I make when I don't have control over the sounds I make. In the film *Notting Hill*, Julia Roberts' character makes fun of Hugh Grant's for saying, "Whoops a daisy." Well, Julia, as it turns out, I make similar inadvertent utterances. If I see someone slip, I instinctively put my hands out and actually say, "Whoops." I've written "Whoops" in stories. But it so happens, that is the *actual* sound I make when I see someone slip or start to fall.

And when I see a president that I sort of idolize, I now know that I say, out loud and in what you might consider an un-James Bondy way, "Oh my gosh."

"Hey there," an agent said to me.

"Hey!" I semi-shouted, realizing that with my inadvertent volume I'd lost my up-to-that-moment carefully cultivated MI6 air, and dropping it more quickly with every breath. "Oh my gosh, hey. I, I just . . ." and then I lifted the empty bucket, using it as the oddest of backstage passes. Feeling the need to explain to the impeccably suited man with a stone cold demeanor my trembling hands and flushed face I said, with the bucket still raised awkwardly high, "You have no idea what this means to me, to be standing in a room with him, I'm just, I mean I've got to get this ice, I'm sorry to bother you I know you're working and protecting and, honestly, a little scary . . . but oh my gosh it's the honor of my life to be in this room right now . . . I made a joke about pat downs earlier and thought they might throw me out . . . then I asked the guy about aliens but really, I'm just thrilled to be standing here, oh my gosh."

From close enough to touch him (which I sensed might be a mistake, given the intensity with which it seemed the agent was now watching me) I looked on as Obama flashed his very famous, very uplifting, very genuine smile around the small space. When the glare of the Secret Service became too much, I proceeded to scoop ice more slowly and carefully than I ever had, soaking up every possible moment to listen to Obama chat with the few people in the room. He joked and laughed with the humor and warmth I'd always known he'd have, even were I to one day find myself in the extremely unlikely situation of being with him in an ice machine room.

Throughout the night, I'd go in and out of the theater and stand at the side to watch Barack watching the show. I know that sounds weird, but I couldn't help it. It brought me such joy to see him bobbing his head in time to the music, clearly captivated by the performance.

The President would come again, months later, to see *Hamilton*. This time, I was familiar with some of the Secret Service agents, and was way cooler around them, making at least a few less ridiculous jokes. And that night, Barack gave a speech after the show. As I stood beside an agent in an entryway to the theater space no more than fifty feet from the president, I got to hear him repeat those world-changing, personally life-altering words, "Yes we can."

And I believed him.

No matter what happens at *Hamilton*, whatever remarkable experiences my silly little job might bring, hearing Obama say, in person and close enough to see the nuance of his every expression, "Yes we can," is probably the one I'll tell my grandchildren about most often.

My grandchildren are going to be *so tired* of hearing about how grandpa once spent time with the best president we've ever had, during the run of the best show ever created.

And almost found out about aliens.

Over the course of my years working for the Nederlander theaters, I'd been keeping something of a public journal on social media. That's where the above story

23

(and all dated material that follows) comes from. I'd had lots of interesting inter-actions bartending on Broadway, and often wrote about them, and other things going on in my life. And it's a good thing I did, because, though I speculated when writing above that being in a room with Barack would probably be my most told story, that turned out to be just the beginning of the wondrous set of experiences *Hamilton* would bring.

Here's my entry from the following day:

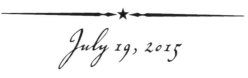

July 19, 2015

Big day yesterday. Got to see the President. And here's what I learned—the Secret Service doesn't have much of a sense of humor whilst on the job. I mean I made some great jokes. *Great* ones! Not even a lip quiver. Then last night, I met Chris Hayes, one of the brightest people on television (not a particularly high bar, as he reminded me when I said the same to him). I had no idea, but Chris told me that he directed Lin in his first play when they went to high school together!

All of this fervor had come from a show that was technically still in rehearsal. During a show's preview period, things continue to get tweaked and reworked and discovered. Therefore, I would constantly find reasons to be in my office early, cleaning a storage shelf that I'd just cleaned, rearranging menu displays and rearranging them back—doing whatever it took to be in the theater and get the chance to witness even the slightest glimpse of Lin's creative process.

At times, rehearsal would be going on in the lobby in front of my bar while the crew worked on technical issues on stage. To be able to listen to Lin say a line to himself, and then repeat it, finding variations each time, in both rhythm and rhymes, until it hit his ears as perfect, felt like watching Michelangelo sculpt, chipping away a beat he didn't need here, smoothing an edge there, slowly releasing the form only he could hear. Over the course of the preview month, Lin poked and prodded the language and tempos until he'd coaxed everything he could from each couplet. Finally, he carved away the final bits of sound and silence concealing his David, and revealed a masterpiece.

It was time to let the critics weigh in, as the show was "locked," and presented to history.

ACT 1, SCENE 4

SHOWTIME

"Wanna take a ride?"

—CARL SAGAN,
CONTACT

On August 6th, 2015, *Hamilton; An American Musical* officially opened. It was an experience unlike any I'd had before. At intermission, the lobby was absolutely pulsing with energy. *Hamilton* was everything people thought it was going to be, and then some. The star-studded audience went wild as the cast took their bows, and the curtain came down on history. Now, it was time to celebrate.

Normally, opening night parties can be rather tense affairs, as everyone involved with the production awaits the posting of reviews. A bad critical reception from the New York Times can be very damaging to a show's prospects, and even spell its doom. But there was no such worry on this night. The only question was *how* good the reviews would be. Articles with phrases like "Supremely executed" and "Blazing inventiveness" and "A triumph" were shared from person to person on phone screens, as what we already knew had now been roundly acknowledged; *Hamilton* was unlike anything anyone had ever seen on Broadway, and would one day mark the place in history where something new and wonderful began, the fork in the road that altered the direction of theater, lifting it from the sea of new entertainment options and placing it again in a station of prominence, reminding us that there are some things only live theater can do.

Lin and the producers threw an opening night gala like no other. After the show, double-decker shuttle buses were waiting to take us to the location of the party on the Hudson River, and as we made our way to them through the tight and bustling crowd, Marie bumped into Jake Gyllenhaal. She looked up into his eyes, hoping this would be the "meet cute" that would one day begin the long story of "them," but his rather annoyed countenance thwarted any such hope.

"Sorry, Jake Gyllenhaal," I said, not ever imaging those would be words I'd one day find the need to say. We left his icy stare behind and headed to the Hudson.

One of the perks of my job is often getting invited to these opening night events, and so I've been to many. But none compared to this. The production spared no expense, throwing the most lavish party I'd ever attended. The Roots provided the live music as the crowd danced, and the question, "Oh my gosh, is that . . . ?" was met with "Yes" after "Yes!" "Yes, we *are* dancing with Lucy Liu and Sally Field!" Lin got up on stage and improvised a rap (a talent of his of which I was now very well aware), putting into rhythmic, rhymed words what this night was like for him. As fireworks exploded over the Hudson, I watched Susan Sarandon's face intermittently light up in wavering colors. Afterwards, Marie and I, and Jake Gyllenhaal and Ariana DeBose and Sarah Jessica Parker and Marc Jacobs and Lin and the *Hamilton* cast danced the rest of the night away—Marie and I being extra careful not to bump into Jake again. I didn't know if our newly minted friendship could withstand a second bump. Lin took my phone and snapped the following photo just after I'd caught him on the dance floor to thank him for the unparalleled festivities, and the beautiful thing he'd just put into the world:

Once the wild opening was behind us, we settled into a steady cadence of well-known people coming to the show. Everyone wanted to see (and be seen at) *Hamilton*. One evening, a rumor was going around the theater that United States Supreme Court Justice Anthony Kennedy was coming. About three months before, Kennedy had written the majority opinion in the Obergefell v. Hodges ruling. This decision required every state to issue marriage licenses to same-sex couples, essentially making marriage a guaranteed right, no matter the sex of the people involved. Here is the final paragraph of Justice Kennedy's opinion:

No union is more profound than marriage, for it embodies the highest ideals of love, fidelity, devotion, sacrifice, and family. In forming a marital union, two people become something greater than once they were. As some of the petitioners in these cases demonstrate, marriage embodies a love that may endure even past death. It would misunderstand these men and women to say they disrespect the idea of marriage. Their plea is that they do respect it, respect it so deeply that they seek to find its fulfillment for themselves. Their hope is not to be condemned to live in loneliness, excluded from one of civilization's oldest institutions. They ask for equal dignity in the eyes of the law. The Constitution grants them that right.

It is so ordered.

So when, during a very busy intermission, I saw him standing beside my bar talking to the house manager, I stopped what I was doing and told my customer I'd be right back—I was not going to let this opportunity pass. I posted the following as soon as intermission ended:

————————————★————————————

September 18, 2015

Tonight, I got to personally thank Justice Kennedy (who authored the majority opinion on the marriage equality decision). I told him that I'd never teared up at a Supreme Court ruling, until reading his final paragraph. I took his hand in both of mine, as he said, "Oh . . . thank you."

What a cool moment.

————————————★————————————

It might interest you to know that I found out later that the man whose hand I grasped with relish and shook with no little degree of passion was not Justice Kennedy. We had been told that Kennedy might be attending that evening, and apparently, through the haze of joy that steps towards equality generate, all older white men look the same to me. This man was not Justice Kennedy, but actually a member of the Nederlander family—the family that owns the theater—which means he must have been very confused when this stranger stopped serving drinks during a busy intermission to come over to him to share his feelings on the recent Supreme Court marriage equality ruling, though he politely accepted the share nonetheless. Whoops.

The *Hamilton* mania continued, and even swelled, day after day. I would constantly look up to see someone I adored, usually for either the creative gifts they've given to the world, or the positive change I'd felt they'd made. Whenever I met these folks, I made it a point to try and let them know, albeit briefly, what they'd meant to me (whether they were who I thought they were or not). When Mark Ruffalo came to the bar, I thanked him for his activism, as well as his talent. Amy Poehler I thanked for all of the laughs and insight, and Spike Lee for his indefatigable voice of social consciousness. When Harrison Ford came, I said, "Hey, I was a carpenter just like you before I began to lead this glamorous life as a bartender—our stories are so similar, man!" "Yeah. Alright yeah," he replied with a smile.

As I would later write:

March 8, 2016

Han Solo and Indiana Jones walked into a bar . . . and it was mine!

That was pretty neat.

Hamilton was on a rocket-like trajectory toward transcendence, and quickly became a part of popular culture in a way no other Broadway show had. I hadn't realized it at first, but I'd been given, purely by chance, a perspective to the birth of a zeitgeist-shifting event that few shared. I had a front row seat as the phenomenon that is *Hamilton* captured the country's attention. And its heart.

Soon, jokes were being made on popular television shows about how difficult it was to get tickets, and it was true. Even before it opened on Broadway, the show had sold out well into the future. Night after night, though, people with pull were somehow getting seats.

Some cast members wanted to know who was in the house for any given performance, while others most definitely did not, preferring not to be distracted, for instance, by the thought that their idol, Beyoncé, would be seated in the second row—right behind Paul McCartney. Quite often, these high-profile guests would want to visit with the cast following the show, so they'd linger behind to greet them on stage or in their dressing rooms. One of the marvelous aspects of my job was the option to stay afterwards and meet some of these folks. We'd mill around chatting on stage, me attempting to stay cool, like *"I just want you to know this is no big deal to me, Jay Z, don't let my trembling fool you,"* while Jay Z and J. Lo and Julie Andrews, Jon Bon Jovi (all the Js, really) and Tom Hanks and Oprah kindly took picture after picture with those gathered. After doing so, they'd exit through the stage door where throngs of admirers, hundreds of them, were waiting behind barricades for the slim chance of getting an autograph or photo with cast members and the various celebrities. I once got the most brief of glimpses into what it's like to be one of those celebrities.

I almost always exit through the main doors of the theater (not wanting too much attention from the bartender groupies), but on one occasion I was backstage for something, and the stage door was the quickest exit. I said goodbye to the security guard and pushed the door, forgetting about the assembled masses. As soon as it swung open, a roar went up from the crowd and cameras began to flash. In that instant, I knew what it must be like to be able to bring such joy to people simply by showing up. Just by being there, you alter how they feel. What an extraordinary thing that must be. Then, in the next moment I felt a mixture of embarrassment for myself, and them. I could almost hear the progression; "Oh my gosh, it's!!! . . . it's!! . . . oh wow that's! . . . wait, is that? . . . I don't think . . . no, that's . . . that's no one. He's no one. Put your camera down." Then, I think they felt sort of badly about me realizing they were realizing I was "no one," and they wanted me to feel like someone, so they cheered again as I said, "Thank you folks, thank you . . . I know I make a mean gin and tonic, but I didn't realize it was that mean. Thank you!" Then, they laughed.

And deleted the photos of me they'd just taken.

I posted the following right after my fifteen-seconds of almost feeling famous:

I just exited through the stage door at *Hamilton* (I usually leave through the front doors) and got a huge ovation from the large crowd waiting for autographs. I had no idea bartenders were such a big deal! To all my fans there tonight, thank you for waiting for me out in the cold. And it was so nice of you to take my suggestion and stay behind after I left to also meet Lin. I'm sure that made him feel good.

It was fun being around all of the hoopla. And, my, was there hoopla. So much so that even the most trivial detail was being mined for something a news outlet could publish. Here's how you know a show has reached another level of public interest; People Magazine wants to interview the bar manager about "his" *Hamilton* cocktails. Over the years, I'd certainly let myself imagine I might be successful at something one day, and not always living in a 4 and-a-half bedroom apartment with seven people and one bathroom. But never did I guess the thing I'd someday have people sticking microphones in my face to hear more about would be "my" hundred-year old drink recipes, rebranded with *Hamilton*-related names. Don't tell People, please; they think my "Founders' Fizz" (just a good-ole Gin Fizz) is an inspired new entry into the cocktail lexicon.

So hungry for any story at all that involved *Hamilton*, news outlets (that instantly found me in some way I still don't understand) began to contact me just moments after I posted the following:

———— ★ ————

March 19, 2016

Amy Schumer. What a lady. What a sweet, beautiful, generous lady.

```
Subtotal:           77.00
TIP_____1,000.00_____
TOTAL_____1077.00
SIGNATURE_____
Thank you for dining with us!
Merchant Copy
```

———— ★ ————

About a month before the above picture was taken showing the $1,000 tip she gave us, comedian and actress Amy Schumer came to *Hamilton* for the first time at the Richard Rodgers Theater. She waited until intermission was over to use the bathroom, meaning the second act had started and the lobby was empty. She walked up to the bar and asked if it was too late to get a drink. "Of course not," Richard, one of our bartenders, responded. We then proceeded to chat with Amy for about ten minutes as the sonorous strains of *Hamilton* provided a score to our conversation. See, Amy was a bartender back in the day, and she knows that many are artists of some kind, paying their dues before finding their way. Amy was funny and dirty and real. She was sweet and kind, spending just as much energy on the three bartenders now gathered to speak with her, as she would have had she been on an evening talk show. We were just as important as anyone else, cameras rolling or not. Before leaving, she put eighty dollars down on the bar for her one drink, and turned away heading back to her seat.

"Please," we said, "this is too much!"

"Good luck with everything," she said with a smile.

During her following visit she left the $1,000 tip on a $77 tab. We took photos of the receipt and posted them to Facebook and Instagram, wanting to share Amy's generosity with our friends. Then, literally within minutes, I was getting emails from producers and reporters asking for interviews. It was a lot of silly fun, as friends called me from around the country when spots moved beyond the local New York stations to national outlets like Good Morning America and Inside Edition and the like. I posted the following to keep family and friends up-to-date on how I was handling my newfound notoriety:

March 21, 2016

I need to go buy some bread. I wonder how many paparazzi are waiting for me downstairs. Listen friends, please don't treat me any differently now that I'm very, very famous. Okay? Please. I'm still the same guy. I still eat bread. Just like you. I didn't realize it until now, but it's true . . . we stars are just like you. And all we ask is the space to just go get some bread in peace every once in a while.

> *Edit: There were surprisingly few paparazzi waiting for me down-stairs. It was close to zero, actually. And it was closer to zero than to one, you might say.*

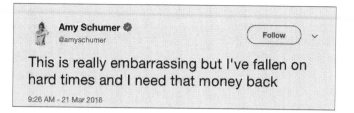

Amy Schumer ✓
@amyschumer
Follow ∨

This is really embarrassing but I've fallen on hard times and I need that money back

9:26 AM - 21 Mar 2016

Amy tweeted the above the following day, but it turned out she wasn't entirely finished. Though the story of that big tip went viral, here's what people don't know: Amy came to see *Hamilton* again a few months later, this time with her sister. I didn't see her on the way in, to my disappointment—I'd wanted to give a proper "Thank you" for her generosity. But Intermission came and went, and still I caught no sight of her. *It's not to be, this time,* I thought. And then, as I described in the post below, this happened:

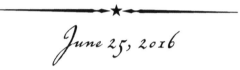

June 25, 2016

After intermission, I started to break down the bar, cleaning and putting things away. I was kneeled down at the refrigerator when I saw a head appear over the bar. I popped up and said, "Hi there! What can I getcha?"

"A water, please," she said.

"Sure. That's five dollars."

I quickly handed it to her, swiped her credit card and said, "Thanks," as I continued my chores. I wasn't going to have her wait for the receipt to print and sign, as the show had started, and no one should miss a second of *Hamilton*. Not for a $5 water. When I looked up a moment later, though, the young lady was still standing there.

"Did you need something else?" I asked. "Oh no. I just wanted to give you a tip." "Oh wow!" I said. "It's a generous woman who misses some of *Hamilton* to give a bartender a tip on a bottle of water." She smiled as I handed her the receipt, saying, "Enjoy the rest of the show," and kneeling back down to continue putting things away in the refrigerator. When I finished a few minutes later, I got back up to find the receipt on the bar.

Amy, wanting to avoid attention this time, had sent her sister to get her a bottle of water—and leave a $2,000 tip.

Of course, the real gift Amy gave doesn't fit on a tip line, and lasts far longer than anything that could. I won't remember what I did with my portion of her financial generosity, but never will I forget the laughs and kindness provided by her generosity of spirit.

———————————★————————————

The parade of patrons from every echelon and type of fame went on. Night after night I found myself oscillating between being awestruck and giddy, as people that have long been a part of my life, for just a moment, actually stepped into it. Here's a small sample of those politicians, athletes and actors who briefly entered . . .

April 8, 2016

We've had celebrities of the highest visibility at *Hamilton*. And the President. And yet, I've never seen anything like the reaction to Bernie Sanders tonight. Watching him handle the crowd, being right in the middle of it, was amazing. Running for president elicits such strong feelings from people. To be able to remain serene at the center of all of that energy is something to behold.

Afterwards, I got to meet him on the *Hamilton* stage, where, in a very positive sign for my Bernie-supporting friends, I witnessed an interaction he had.

One of the "Real Housewives" was at *Hamilton,* as well. Being introduced to Sanders after the show, Bernie looked confused. His wife then whispered in his ear, telling him, I assume, who she was. To which Bernie quietly responded, "Who?"

Apparently, actual reality leaves no time for "reality" TV in Bernie's schedule.

April 9, 2016

I didn't realize I was nearly as tall as Derek Jeter and Dave Winfield. I really should have stuck with baseball.

April 23, 2016

Rosie O'Donnell is a big fan of *Hamilton*, and comes often. Today, as two young girls (probably about fourteen) were ordering some soda and candy at the bar, Rosie came up;

> **ROSIE:** *"Their stuff is on me."*
> **GIRLS:** (blank stares)
> **ROSIE** (smiling)**:** *"I'm Rosie O'Donnell."*
> **GIRLS:** (blanker stares)
> **ROSIE:** (Exquisite Pause. Exquisite Pause. Exquisite Pause) *"Tell your mother Rosie O'Donnell bought your Junior Mints."*

ACT 1, SCENE 5

SOMETHING TO BE A PART OF

"When my cue comes, call me."

—WILLIAM SHAKESPEARE
A MIDSUMMER NIGHT'S DREAM

Hamilton had become an absolute juggernaut. Every time a new batch of tickets opened up, they sold out within minutes. It wasn't long before the earliest tickets you could get from the box office were many months into the future, which meant that if one wanted to see the show right away, they had to go to the secondary market where tickets were selling for enormously inflated prices—sometimes thousands of dollars each. Lin and *Hamilton's* lead producer, Jeffrey Seller, wanted to make the show accessible to as many people as possible, and it was decided that there would be a daily lottery. You would just come by the theater, put your name in, and later that day ten names would be drawn. Those people would get $10 front row seats to the most popular show Broadway had ever seen. Hundreds of people began showing up to the lottery drawing, and Lin didn't want the vast majority of them who would not win to go away empty-handed. So, he and Tommy Kail decided to put on a small daily show for the enormous crowds that were now gathering, eventually getting so big they were nearly shutting down 46th street in midtown Manhattan. They called the program "Ham4Ham," and it soon became almost as big a hit as the show itself. People were coming just to see the short performance, the lottery tickets a secondary thought. What is amazing is that it was something different every day. Lin, as I've mentioned, is a savant. His brain works much faster, in some ways, than the average brain. On top of keeping up with all of the enormous publicity *Hamilton* was now garnering, making countless media appearances, as well as playing the title role in the show seven times per week, Lin, with Tommy's help, was daily coming up with a new performance for the Ham4Ham series. He'd often showcase individual talents of cast members, and soon brought in other Broadway performers to sing a song or do a skit of some kind. Then, one day, one of the bartenders tweeted at Lin asking for him to involve us. To which Lin replied, "Let's do it."

And six months later, we did.

Many of the bartenders, merchandise staff, stage hands and cast members play on the *Hamilton* softball team, so Lin decided to do a song from Damn Yankees as the Ham4Ham performance. As I was sitting in my office, someone came in and said, "Hey, here's the sheet music. Lin wants to rehearse with you guys tomorrow before the show." Which prompted no small degree of anxiety . . .

May 31, 2016

I was told today that I need to be on stage at noon tomorrow to rehearse with Lin.

Lin-Manuel Miranda.

Who has been nominated for all the Tony awards and recently won the MacArthur "genius grant."

That Lin.

So, I'm currently in the market for a vocal coach. That works late night, and can see me now through noon tomorrow.

And is capable of miracle working.

The following day I headed into the theater for a musical rehearsal which Lin would be directing, with Alex Lacamoire providing accompaniment. I lost sleep thinking about singing in front of Lin, but having Alex there added a few more beads of sweat, as he isn't your everyday accompanist: Alex is a TONY and

Grammy Award winning Orchestrator and Musical Director, performing those roles for both *In the Heights* and *Hamilton*, among others, and co-arranger of *Hamilton's* score. He came in and sat in the chair right beside me, which instantaneously and dramatically increased my perspiration output. He's an extremely nice person, I'm thrilled to report, and perhaps noticing my glistening forehead said, "This is gonna be fun!" Which made it so.

Lin rhythmically slapped his knee as he and Alex worked out the beat, and I rubbed my eyes to make certain I was awake. *Was I actually being directed, if only for one day, by the Sondheim of our time, Lin-Manuel Miranda? Could this be real?* When the doors to the theater opened to the multitudes gathered outside, and they erupted in immediate applause, it was clear that it was; I was singing on Broadway. Well, not inside a Broadway theater, as I'd once upon a time imagined, but literally on Broadway.

Like, out on the street.

———————— ★ ————————

June 1st, 2016

Ham4Ham has featured the likes of Audra MacDonald and Kelli O'Hara. Matthew Morrison. Brian d'arcy James. Billy Porter and Norm Lewis.
And me.

#oneofthesethingsisnotliketheothers

———————— ★ ————————

Sitting in the theater that day, with Alex Lacamoire to my left, and Lin leaning against the chair immediately in front of me directing us on the Ham4Ham performance, I was suddenly thrust back in time. The last time I'd been in a musical rehearsal was in high school, when, to my great surprise, my unsinging self somehow got cast as the "Narrator" and "Mysterious Man" in *Into the Woods*. I found myself in that long ago auditorium where so much of my life began, looking at Pat Souney, the larger than life director who was introducing us to the power of theater as she stormed up on stage to ask me precisely what I thought I was doing when I'd decided to go off script and ad lib for the amusement of my friends. "This is not a joke," she thundered. "You are not here for yourself! You are here for *us*. Theater is sacred. It is a tool that changes who we are, and what the world is." Pat made more than one person cry during those high school rehearsals, but through those tears deep insight became visible. But she made every single one of us think. No student of Pat's left that program without a profound respect for theatre, and what it is capable of.

As Lin waved his finger in time, urging the group of mostly stage hands, bartenders and ushers in front of him to find the beat, I came back into the room and marveled at the moment I was having. One of the greatest musical minds in humanity's history had his hand on my shoulder, saying, "This is going to be great!" *If Pat could only see me now*, I thought.

We went up on stage for one final run-through of the song, and I looked down at the now famous turn-table I was standing on, upon which *Hamilton's* exquisite choreography unfolds, and then out into the big, beautiful, Broadway house, admiring the view the *Hamilton* cast gets every night from their side of the curtain. The side that used to be mine.

And that's when I noticed it.

As we got ready for the doors to open onto 46th street for our Ham4Ham performance, I was surprised to find that beneath the excitement was . . . a sadness. Don't get me wrong; I thoroughly enjoyed the moment to "perform" with Lin. But when we'd finished, and went back inside, Lin, and those in the cast that had been with us, took a right, and I took a left. They went backstage to prepare for the real show, and I went back to the bar. Icing up the beer in the sink, I had the thought again; *If Pat could only see me now.*

Later that night, a man who'd literally run from the theater to the bathroom, hoping to miss as little of the show as possible, came up to me before going back in. "This is just incredible," he said after hurriedly ordering a soda. As I poured it, the sound of the carbonated liquid filling the souvenir cup mixed with the sounds of the earth-shaking, Broadway-altering, world-changing masterpiece in the background. Standing so close to where such creativity and joy was unfolding, and people were being moved and stretched and becoming better, in the ways Pat taught us about, I filled a cup with Pepsi. After handing the man his drink, I watched him walk the fifty feet into the theater. And thought about how enormous a difference fifty feet can sometimes make.

I realized then that the sadness I'd noticed that afternoon had been there all the while, lurking just below the exhilaration and fun *Hamilton* had brought.

Two weeks later, *Hamilton* won eleven TONY awards. The following day, Lin came into the lobby with his TONYs for Best Score and Best Musical, and in another inclusive gesture I'd not ever experienced with a show before, he dropped the awards off on the bar so that the house staff could take pictures with them. But no matter how much Lin so kindly wanted us to feel a part of what he'd done, as I held them and smiled, I couldn't help but wish I'd done something to earn the photo.

When Lin and I were children, we both imagined the same sort of life, I'm guessing—one full of meaning, and making a difference.

Now, though, while he was busy making not only a difference, but historically raising the Broadway bar, I was busy behind one, histrionically raising peoples' blood sugar.

Standing but one wall and yet an entire world away from where I hoped I'd one day be, I leaned against the bar and gazed at the TONY awards sitting in front of me, longing to be a "fraction" as useful as Lin, to have a "fragment" of his impact.

ACT 1, SCENE 6

ONE LAST TIME

"We can only be said to be alive in those moments when our hearts are conscious of our treasures."

—THORNTON WILDER,
THE WOMAN OF ANDROS

As the days to Lin's departure ticked away, I began to ever more fully appreciate how lucky I was to have daily experienced his genius.

More and more, I understood what a unique thing it was to watch Lin perform, over and over again in the piece he'd created. Given how well-known Lin's gift had become, it was very clear that he'd soon be pulled in many directions, his brilliance having written him an open ticket for whatever it wanted to pursue next. His time performing in *Hamilton* would be limited, and I felt sorry for the people who'd never get to see him do it in person. I realized that I was witnessing something history would speak of. For a time, I was watching Einstein at his chalkboard in his prime. I was listening to Billie Holiday from the front row of a small Harlem nightclub in 1932, when her vocal virtuosity was largely undiscovered, but apparent to anyone lucky enough to be in the room. I was seeing Shakespeare act seven times per week in his plays (what some people I know would give to go back in time and do that) and hearing what iambic pentameter sounded like out of the mouth of the Bard himself. I was in a time machine moment—one of the moments, hundreds of years from now, you'd want to use your time machine for, even if you only had limited opportunities (because flux capacitors are notoriously unreliable).

By the time Lin's final performance in the Broadway run of *Hamilton* came along, the whole world knew we were witnessing one of the rare Promethean bursts of intellect and creativity that, now and again, light up our lives. It isn't very often that a star of Broadway transcends the medium of theater to enter the rarified air of international stardom. But with Lin, such was the astral nature of

Hamilton, that this is exactly what happened. He was now on morning news shows and late-night talk shows and gracing the covers of check-out line magazines. Lin had landed, and in order to get a glimpse of him playing the titular role in the phenomenon he'd birthed into existence, people, in the last week of his run, were paying thousands of dollars, sometimes as much as ten-thousand, for a single seat. On his final night, Spike Lee came for the eighth time and Rosie O'Donnell for the twenty-fourth, each wanting to see Da Vinci paint the Mona Lisa once more.

It had become abundantly clear to those of us who had watched Lin take the stage more than three-hundred times how remarkably fortunate we were.

July 9, 2016

Today marks Lin's final day in *Hamilton*. To be able to experience nearly every performance has been good for the soul. It reminds me daily what is within us. The good, the love, and the explosion of creativity waiting inside. It yearns to escape, yet so many things keep it too often caged. But when it manages to burst forth—Lin and so many others are evidence of what's possible. Burst, friends. With love. With joy. With life. Burst with that inimitable thing that makes you, and only you, you. Don't be afraid of the power you have. Let yourself out. Because the next *Hamilton* is in someone right now. And you aren't meant to keep it.

Lin's final bow took place on the same day as that of other original cast members, including Phillipa (Pipa) Soo, who so beautifully played Eliza, and Leslie Odom Jr., who won the TONY Award for Best Actor for his deeply layered portrayal of Aaron Burr.

As you might imagine, the scene, as these three were pushed out to the front of the line, was quite an emotional one.

Lin is an enormous fan of Aaron Sorkin and particularly The West Wing. As he told Vulture in 2016 of the hit television show, "It pulls back the curtain on how decision-making happens at the highest level, or at least how you hope it would be. The amount of information Aaron Sorkin packs into a scene gave me this courage to trust the audience to keep up."

As if Lin, Leslie and Pipa coming forward to take their final *Hamilton* curtain call wasn't already emotional enough, as the audience went absolutely wild, refusing to stop applauding, Alex Lacamoire and the orchestra suddenly struck up the West Wing theme song, which came as a total surprise to Lin, and drew tears from many in the theater, myself included.

While this day had been drawing closer, I wondered what might become of the show upon these significant departures. We were losing not only its creator, but also two other integral pieces of the puzzle in Leslie and Phillipa. Would the magic still be there on the following night? Would the heights of theatrical ecstasy that the combination of Lin's writing and the talents of those leaving had occasioned ever be reached again? It was no small relief to discover that, indeed, they would. It became immediately clear at the next performance that it wasn't just this extremely providential, once-in-a-generation coming together of supremely talented individuals that made the show soar—the structural bones of *Hamilton* itself provides the lift. It was a joy to find that what Lin made is a masterpiece because of what it is, and doesn't solely rely on who is in it. The show itself is a star. The show itself is magic.

As such, even after the parting of those three phenomenal actors, *Hamilton's* bull run continued. There was no letup whatsoever in the energy surrounding it, as it continued to attract unheard of attention for a Broadway show. I was daily watching the extraordinary unfold. On top of that, my heretofore under-appreciated job behind the bar continued to introduce me to people I'd always thought would be the ones I'd do anything to meet. Night after night, I found myself talking with people who loomed large in my mind—people who, before *Hamilton*, were mostly two-dimensional representations my imagination had conjured about those that everyone "knew,"—the most recognizable actors and actresses, political figures and musicians, Supreme Court Justices, Presidents and Vice Presidents and presidential candidates. And quite a few famous athletes, too.

It was initially surreal to be standing in the middle of the entire San Antonio Spurs basketball team, for instance, but I began to get used to seeing athletes up close like this, and marveling at how our bodies could be so . . . not similar. In fact, I was daily reminded by the *Hamilton* cast, often rehearsing in the lobby right in front of me, of the range of body types that exist, and the, well, very wide gap, the impossible to overstate gaping gap of all gaps, the chasmist of yawning chasms, between mine and theirs.

September 26, 2016

It's not easy being around Broadway dancers on a daily basis. These people are world class athletes, and I'm, sort of, not that, for the most part. So, I've been trying to be more careful about what I eat, and to exercise more. To that end, there is an organic juice place near the theater that I've been going to. And let me tell you something; it makes you feel pretty healthy when the guy at the organic juice place asks, "The usual?"

But then the guy at the ice cream place asked the same thing.

Luckily, however, my more down to earth, shall we say, less intimidating is how I think we'll put it, body, did not turn out to be a barrier to world-renown.

October 18, 2016

I was just flipping through the Newsweek *Hamilton* Special Edition, and saw my picture. I was really hoping to keep the Nation's attention focused on beating Donald Trump, and not on me. Friends, please don't let me become a distraction. There are more important things than my little face in Newsweek Magazine.

(It's on page 89)

(Right Side)

(Deep in the crease)

(Let me know if you need more help finding it)

Speaking of Donald Trump, all the while that the wonderful *Hamilton* madness was unfolding, the presidential campaigns had been in full swing, and now, the 2016 election was upon us. Though there had been much drama throughout, the ultimate result, to most of the people I was around (and, I daresay, much of the world) never felt as though it was in much doubt. I was confident Hillary Clinton would handily defeat Donald Trump, and that we would continue our steady, though too slow (especially if you are anything other than a cisgendered "straight" person in light skin), march of progress. The alternative was simply too insane, frankly, for me to imagine. There was no way we would elect a person so, just . . . Trumpy.

I mean . . . right?

THE WORLD TURNED UPSIDE DOWN

"A dangerous ambition more often lurks behind the specious mask of zeal for the rights of the people than under the forbidden appearance of zeal for the firmness and efficiency of government. History will teach us that the former has been found a much more certain road to the introduction of despotism than the latter, and that of those men who have overturned the liberties of republics, the greatest number have begun their career by paying an obsequious court to the people; commencing demagogues, and ending tyrants."

—ALEXANDER HAMILTON

Obama's eight years, as you've surely gleaned by now, had gone a long way to helping me feel better about things, and after electing our first person of color, it seemed to me that we were well on our way to electing the first female President of the United States. Donald Trump was running, but that didn't seem like an actual possibility to me. I know we once elected the Terminator as the Governor of California, but the "You're fired!" guy? That just didn't seem remotely like a real thing. *There is no way,* I thought, *we could possibly go from the country that elected a poet, to the country that elected a guy famous for being, basically, a world-class . . .* (here's the Madlibs portion of the proceedings, as you get to pick your own word—I went with "snollygoster"). On top of that, he was now on tape saying things about his treatment of women that I was sure not even the staunchest of the Republican base could possibly abide.

In my mind, we'd busted through an enormous barrier by twice electing Obama, and we were about to do it again. This election was surely going to be about breaking down walls, not putting them up.

But then . . .

Though it did not compare to what I felt on that morning in September of 2001, when it became clear that we had, indeed, elected Donald Trump, I felt sick. The whiplash from Bush to Obama to this guy was just enormous for me. And what it felt like for women and minorities and immigrants . . . well I just couldn't begin to know.

An immigrant himself, Hamilton once wrote in a letter, "Every day proves to me more and more that this American world was not made for me."

Hamilton is famous for its diversity in casting (as I'm sure you're aware, unless you picked up this book by mistake—and if so, you might as well stay, at this point—I mean you've made it to page 57. And there's a big surprise coming on page 262, which you wouldn't want to miss). The fact its casting garnered such a great deal of attention makes quite clear why attempting to make some headway into the far too egregious, for far too long, issue of underrepresentation and non-inclusion on Broadway is important to Lin. The production raises up not only immigrants and people of color, but also women—groups of people, it seemed to me, that Trump's campaign often spoke of in worrying ways. Many people in my own life and in the *Hamilton* cast, who identify with one or more of those categories now found themselves positively reeling from the election. In New York, even, a place known for its diversity, stories of latent and subtle racism boldly coming to the forefront were being told, such as a case where white men shouted out of their cars to minorities on the sidewalk, "Go back home. This is Trump's America now." It wasn't just frightening for the people I work with every day, it was *traumatizing* to know the country had elected someone who seemed to stoke tendencies we saw as racist, misogynistic and xenophobic. The fact that so many had voted for someone who seemed to run on the vilifying of immigrants and belittling opponents and who said women should be punished if they have an abortion and that an entire religion should be banned from the country and who mocked a reporter with a physical disability and urged supporters at his rallies to "knock the crap" out of people with opposing views and compared being gay to using "unattractive" golf clubs—is something most of my friends and I just couldn't wrap our minds around. For many in the *Hamilton* family, from Lin and the creative team to the cast to the producers, it was a very difficult time. As Jeffrey Seller, *Hamilton's* lead producer, said to the New York Times, "Our cast could barely go on stage the day after the election. The election was painful and crushing to all of us here."

But the show must go on, of course, so as we worked through the emotional and psychological fallout from the election, *Hamilton* forged ahead, becoming a bright spot for many in a frightening time.

And things were about to take a turn for the majorly meta.

While, in real life, many of us struggled with the imminent departure of President Obama, *Hamilton* was every day reminding me about the first time a president left office, and the poetry with which he did it. Establishing, perhaps, the most profound aspect of our democracy—the peaceful transition of power from one administration to the next—Washington decided to step away from the highest office in our fledgling land, to not seek another term in the next election, which he surely would have handily won. A brand-new nation, still finding its footing, still wobbly on its spindly legs, was unready to see this pillar of its founding leave, fearful the foundation was not yet secure, and susceptible to collapse. Seeking to quell the worries of a nascent country, Washington, with Hamilton's help, penned a remarkable farewell address—an address that would set the tone for the next two-hundred years of presidential farewells. Hearing the poetry of the final paragraphs, Lin wove Washington's words into one of the most moving scenes of the show, "One Last Time."

This number always gets me. I don't walk out of the theater with dry eyes any time I watch it. But on this night, watching Chris Jackson sing "One Last Time," one last time, I would lose any slight grasp on composure I may have weakly held.

Chris has been a part of Lin's creative journey going all the way back to Freestyle Love Supreme. The first time I saw him was during that rehearsal of *In the Heights* when I discovered the Cup Guy's true identity. Chris was an absolute powerhouse on stage, an actor of substantial gravitas, and with a voice to match. On top of that, he was just a really great guy. The first time I met him, he'd been sitting on the steps drinking a cup of coffee in the back alley of the Rodgers that lead to the dressing rooms. Our ice machine is located back there as well, and as I passed him with two empty buckets I said, "It's been a lot of fun watching you up there."

"Oh thanks! It's been the thrill of my life," he said.

After I finished filling the two ice buckets, and began to make my way back to the lobby, he grabbed one and said, "Let me help you with that." And in that moment made a lifelong fan.

Chris' portrayal of "Benny" in *In the Heights* was an enormous amount of fun, but his George Washington in *Hamilton* (a role Lin wrote with Chris and his strengths in mind) was truly something to behold. Losing him, while we were in the midst of losing Obama, hit me hard on this night, and it fell to a young lady to pick me back up, as I wrote about later that evening:

November 14, 2016

Chris Jackson, who plays George Washington, is a force of nature. I first met him years ago during *In the Heights*, when his voice and easy charm (and offer to help me carry a bucket of ice) made me an instant admirer. To see him embody Washington in *Hamilton* has been a true joy. I feel sorry for the actor who has to step into the part next, which will happen tomorrow, as this evening was Chris' final performance in the role he originated.

Every time he came on stage tonight, I ran into the theater, wanting to soak in every last moment of his unsurpassable portrayal. And as Chris, with red, wet eyes, finished "One Last Time" tonight, for the last time (which engendered a full minute-long standing O in the middle of the show), I lost the last vestige of dignity I was trying to hold on to when I rushed back to the bar and had to tearily inform a thirteen-year-old girl that we were out of Pepsi.

"Oh, it's okay!" She comfortingly said. "Sprite is fine! Don't cry!"

This has been a rough week.

But, gosh, there's great stuff in this world. Like Chris Jackson's George Washington. And that sweet, empathetic thirteen-year-old girl.

Here are the words that most spoke to Lin from Washington's address, and that he included in the show:

> *Though, in reviewing the incidents of my administration, I am unconscious of intentional error, I am nevertheless too sensible of my defects not to think it probable that I may have committed many errors. Whatever they may be, I fervently beseech the Almighty to avert or mitigate the evils to which they may tend. I shall also carry with me the hope that my country will never cease to view them with indulgence; and that, after forty-five years of my life dedicated to its service with an upright zeal, the faults of incompetent abilities will be consigned to oblivion, as myself must soon be to the mansions of rest.*

Relying on its kindness in this as in other things, and actuated by that fervent love towards it, which is so natural to a man who views in it the native soil of himself and his progenitors for several generations, I anticipate with pleasing expectation that retreat in which I promise myself to realize, without alloy, the sweet enjoyment of partaking, in the midst of my fellow-citizens, the benign influence of good laws under a free government, the ever-favorite object of my heart, and the happy reward, as I trust, of our mutual cares, labors, and dangers.

How could it possibly be, I wondered, that in just two-hundred short years, we'd gone from a president who wrote words like that, to one that said, when asked about gay marriage, things like this:

"It's like in golf. . . A lot of people—I don't want this to sound trivial—but a lot of people are switching to these really long putters, very unattractive . . . It's weird. You see these great players with these really long putters, because they can't sink three-footers anymore. And I hate it. I am a traditionalist."

For those I lived and worked with every day, this comparison of a basic right to people using "weird" putters that are "unattractive" while golfing spoke deeply of the person we'd just elected. Moving from a president that had the White House splashed in the colors of the rainbow on the night the marriage equality ruling came down from the Supreme Court, to one who said the above, was a swing of the pendulum a world too far back in the opposite direction.

Hamilton is about the birth of America, a time the world had been "turned upside down," a line that legend tells us the bested and bewildered British soldiers, members of the mightiest fighting machine the world had ever known, sang, after laying down their arms in surrender while being paraded out of town by the ragtag, yet somehow victorious, Continental Army. It's something that is difficult to imagine, a history-altering event like that, even when depicted by world-class story-tellers. It feels so far off, so very distant, that its reality is blurred. We glimpse it through the lens of time, which, like a filter, sifts out the rough spots, leaving mostly the poetry behind. But suddenly, we didn't need stunning depictions of centuries past to understand what those British soldiers might have been feeling, since, just a week before this, the world, *our* world, ours right then and there, had been turned upside down by the election.

We'd all been watching the unfolding flip from afar on the news with everyone else. But suddenly it was here, at our doorstep. In our lobby. Standing, in fact, just feet away. With little warning, we were brought face to face with what had felt like a reality show, a B-level movie where a character, so shallowly written that he's almost a cartoon, becomes the leader of the free world.

But Mike Pence, the character's loyal sidekick, was all too real, standing there in the heavy silence. The sound of his breathing and the look on his too close face shattered, perhaps, the last hopes we'd been holding that this was just a terrible nightmare. It wasn't. This was real. And we were going to need to deal with it.

It's Hard to Listen to You with a Straight Face

"The sacred rights of mankind are not to be rummaged for among old parchments or musty records. They are written, as with a sunbeam, in the whole volume of human nature, by the Hand of Divinity itself, and can never be erased or obscured by mortal power."

—Alexander Hamilton

It was the quietest I'd ever experienced the lobby of the Richard Rodgers theater to be. When the lights flashed, signaling that the show was about to begin, no one moved. Normally, the flickering kicked the full and already bustling lobby into an even more elevated state of excitement (and slight panic) as patrons buying last-minute drinks and hurriedly using the too few bathrooms began to race towards their seats, the direction of which the panic had often erased the memory of, bumping into one another on the way, then easily forgiving each other since everyone understood the stakes; *Hamilton* was about to begin, and after the great effort it took to get tickets and finally be in "The room where it happens," to miss even a second was an unacceptable thought. So, when the lights flashed, people would instinctively run—the direction an almost insignificant detail. They just knew they needed to get inside. Any door would do.

I witnessed this near hysteria eight times a week.

But on this night, the flashing lights were a mere formality, a rote following of duties since the audience had already been seated and, but for a few people, the lobby was empty. In the heavy stillness stood me, my coworkers, and flanked on either side by a Secret Service agent, the Vice President-elect of the United States, Mike Pence. The silence was palpable. It was so void of sound, in fact, that the library-soft crying of the friend standing beside me was all I could hear. I looked to my right to find tears streaming down her cheek.

While my friend wept, I looked at Pence, and he at me, and my mind began to race, trying to find a right way to handle this one moment in time. The fingers at the end of my folded arms caught a button I was wearing on my vest. A button that, I suddenly realized, contained the only response I needed. The pin had been made for the *Hamilton* staff after Lin gave a now famous acceptance speech when winning the Best Score TONY earlier in the year.

Rather than improvising his remarks, as had been his wont after receiving similar awards in the past, coming to the microphone he said, "I'm not free-styling. I'm too old." Instead, he pulled a folded page from his pocket, upon which he'd penned lines earlier that day after learning of the shooting at a gay nightclub in Orlando, in which fifty people had been lost. The sonnet, which speaks of the love he has for his wife, Vanessa, a love that is sacred and meant for all, quickly became a sensation:

> *My wife's the reason anything gets done.*
> *She nudges me towards promise by degrees.*
> *She is a perfect symphony of one.*
> *Our son is her most beautiful reprise.*
> *We chase the melodies that seem to find us*
> *Until they're finished songs and start to play.*
> *When senseless acts of tragedy remind us*
> *That nothing here is promised, not one day.*
> *This show is proof that history remembers.*
> *We live through times when hate and fear seem stronger.*
> *We rise and fall and light from dying embers,*
> *Remembrances that hope and love last longer.*
> *And love is love is love is love is love is love is love*
> *Cannot be killed or swept aside.*
> *I sing Vanessa's symphony, Eliza tells her story.*
> *Now fill the world with music, love, and pride.*

A week or so after the TONYS, the pin I still wore was made. On it were Lin's two simple, repeated words: "Love is love is love is love is love is love is love is love."

From what I've read, Mike Pence doesn't appear to believe that love is love in the same sense that I do. He is said to be a very religious man (depending on what that word means to you), and from interpretations of

words written thousands of years ago involving people of the same sex "lying together" being an "abomination," has taken a staunchly anti-gay stance. Since, for him, those sentences put to paper millennia ago are the word of his God, he seems to feel it's important for one to do whatever one can to stem the flow of love between two people with certain bodies. (I don't know how Pence feels about people with flat noses or crooked backs or a broken foot not being allowed to enter a church, which is another rule found in the same book, but logic would say he must be on top of this with the same zeal).

A statement on the website for his congressional campaign in 2000 read as follows:

"Congress should support the reauthorization of the Ryan White Care Act only after completion of an audit to ensure that federal dollars were no longer being given to organizations that celebrate and encourage the types of behaviors that facilitate the spreading of the HIV virus. Resources should be directed toward those institutions which provide assistance to those seeking to change their sexual behavior."

The Ryan White Care Act provides federal funding for patients with HIV/AIDS. What Pence meant by "organizations that celebrate and encourage the types of behaviors that facilitate the spreading of the HIV virus," isn't entirely clear, but many people, myself included, suspect the "behavior" he refers to is sex, specifically, sex between people with the same reproductive organs. However, HIV can be spread via sex between heterosexual partners, as well. So, sex itself is a behavior that facilitates the spreading of the HIV virus. It isn't clear if Pence thinks sex, in general, is a no-no. What is clear is that he wanted to reroute money from a program aiming to treat and reduce the transmission of HIV to, instead, institutions that are trying to make people who are gay not gay, something the scientific community currently, and finally, sees as impossible. You can't, our current science tells us, *think* yourself gay or *think* yourself not gay—no matter how many electric shocks are sent through the system.

It appears that if you are gay, Mike Pence thinks you are "unnatural" and that your love is perhaps not as worthy as his love—an "abomination," even.

So, just imagine if you aren't gay, what it would be like if you *were* gay, and you had to look into his eyes, face to face, and be polite about it.

66

On the day that Mike Pence came to *Hamilton*, I found myself standing between two people in that precise situation. Working in theater, I happen to spend my days with a lot of people who are not "straight." Sexual and gender "non-conformity" is woven so thoroughly into the fabric of our lives that it becomes just another part of the tapestry. The theater is a space where those who have grappled for acceptance and equality in these areas often feel relatively safe. But into that comparative comfort, a disruptive agent decidedly not safe had just been dropped.

Upon his arrival, Pence had been spirited to a private area while the rest of the patrons took their seats. As the Secret Service made a final sweep of some kind inside the theatre, he was brought out to the lobby where he now stood along with ten or so members of our staff. With two agents posted just behind him, he smiled at us, getting few back. It was all very awkward, actually—It had been just ten days since we'd been "crushed," as Jeffrey Seller said, by the election. New York City, in general, seemed quieter during those ten days than it usually is, as people tried to process what had just happened. Looking back, I believe we were in shock, and actually grieving. And the quiet that had filled the city streets during those ten days, was now concentrated in the small space of that theater lobby. It was the loudest silence I've ever been a part of. Standing to my left was a young gay man, and to my right was Christine. Christine (whose pronouns are she/her/hers, in case you ever meet her) identifies as queer, and she and I have been close for many years. As she stood there with Pence just fifteen feet away, unprepared for how difficult this moment would be for her, tears began to stream down her face. After a few minutes of this tense, portrait-like stillness, one of the agents received a message in his ear and gave a nod, while beginning to guide the Vice President-elect towards his seat. To get there, he needed to walk past us through the narrow space. As he approached, his gaze skipped quickly past my weeping friend and landed on me, perhaps sensing the best chance he had between me and the two friends to my sides at finding someone happy to meet him, and he began to raise his hand to wave or perhaps shake mine.

I tend to be a very congenial person. It is nearly impossible for me to be impolite to someone who is being polite to me. Pence was looking into my eyes and smiling, and in that moment he became a human being. In the weeks that preceded, I saw him and his boss as so awful that they felt like the "bad guys" out of a children's story. They might as well have been wearing skull and crossbones eye patches and wielding bright red light sabers as they scorched the earth in low, breathy tones. People, of course, are almost never really like that. That easily summed up. We're incomprehensible bundles of thoughts and ideas and feelings and pasts and hopes and desires and dimensions we aren't set up to fully perceive in others. We're almost all good sometimes, and not so at others, and though it's easy to see the bad, we can have a hard time understanding what put it there. There's a great word I recently learned that speaks to this notion: "Sonder." It's a new word coined by John Koenig in his "The Dictionary of Obscure Sorrows." He defines it thusly:

Sonder

n. *the realization that each random passerby is living a life as vivid and complex as your own—populated with their own ambitions, friends, routines, worries and inherited craziness—an epic story that continues invisibly around you like an anthill sprawling deep underground, with elaborate passageways to thousands of other lives that you'll never know existed, in which you might appear only once, as an extra sipping coffee in the background, as a blur of traffic passing on the highway, as a lighted window at dusk.*

In the moment Mike Pence was smiling at me, I experienced sonder, and he became a real person with a real life, and with "inherited craziness," wanting to politely interact.

While Christine cried beside me.

My heart pounded and my internal system went into adrenaline-induced haywire, as, against my natural instinct, I didn't reach to shake his hand, but instead pointed at the pin I was wearing.

He looked at it, lowered his arm, read the two simple, repeating words, weakly smiled and moved on. I have no idea if he knew to what the words referred, but I do know he realized I was not on board with whatever part of his unknown-to-me inner life that causes him to alienate and marginalize and wound people who are gay, contributing vast amounts of pain to people I love—people like Christine, who dried her face as he walked away to his orchestra seats.

About forty minutes later, I posted a short description of my interaction with him on Facebook:

★

November 18, 2016

I just had a moment. One of those things you'll remember forever. Mike Pence is at *Hamilton* tonight. After the audience was seated, they ushered him into the lobby to wait as Secret Service did final checks inside the house. I, along with the rest of the staff, stood there with him. In silence. When the all clear was given, he started for his seat. As he came within two feet of me, he smiled his practiced smile and waved at me. I didn't move. Except to point at the pin on my chest. Which says, "Love is love is love is love is love is love is love is love."

★

After he passed us, I ran into the theater from the other side, curious to know how the audience would react, unaware as they were of his presence in the building. When Pence entered the house, the lights were still up, and the audience suddenly saw him. A smattering of claps were immediately answered and soon lost in a louder chorus of "boos," as the question we had been repeatedly asked (but not allowed to answer) "Why is there so much security tonight?" was resolved for the thirteen-hundred theater-goers. And from that moment, the audience remained just as vocal, using every reaction to it as a way to communicate their feelings with the Vice President-elect. "The room where it happens" became the room where it was actually happening, where the rights birthed in the story being told on stage were being expressed in real time. Usually, art takes time for its full effect to be felt. There is a well-known joke about the works of painters, for instance, having little value until the artist is dead. Art weaves its way into our subconscious first, often changing us over time, without us even knowing it. It is the opposite of the frog that gets boiled alive, not noticing the gradual rise in temperature. People don't get better because we are told to. We get better because things, like art, make us better, usually so slowly that we don't realize it's happening.

But on this night, art was making a difference on the spot.

Hamilton is always alive with energy, but never had it been *this* charged. In the most remarkable and electrifying evening of theater I have ever experienced, the audience seemed to quickly, collectively decide they would use the extraordinary opportunity of watching a show about the founding of America, the genesis of a new democracy, while two centuries later, sitting alongside the Vice-President-elect, to demonstrate the fruits of that struggle and send a clear message to him on where the majority of those in the room stood. Every line of the show became powerfully pointed, endowed now, with meta meanings that were lost on no one. By the time the words "Immigrants, we get the job done" were met with an applause so raucous and extended that the next five lines couldn't be heard, every hoot and holler and loud-as-I-can-clap clearly intended as a rebuke to the positions of the President-Elect and New York City native son, Donald Trump, the hair on my neck was standing on end, and tears obscured my vision. I wrote the following during the first act:

> *Tonight, as Mike Pence sits in the audience, the words "Immigrants, we get the job done" leapt from the stage with a special something, and they brought the house down. For a full minute, you couldn't hear the actors, so loud was the applause and hollering from the crowd. I've never been more proud of New York City.*

About twenty minutes following that post, I was serving drinks for intermission. My phone was in my pocket as I worked, and I suddenly felt something I hadn't before; my phone was getting very hot. I could feel it against my leg, and as soon as I had the chance, I took it out, thinking something must be wrong with the battery. But there wasn't. As it turned out, I had been getting thousands of notifications about the Mike Pence posts. Thousands of people were "liking," sharing and commenting on them.

The posts had struck a chord, and I suddenly found myself with a large number of virtual "friends" I didn't know. People, mostly, who had been blindsided by the election, it seemed, and now needed to know they were not alone in that feeling—people who were shaken by what they saw as an enormous step backwards in our cultural evolution, and feared the direction things might be heading.

When Mike Pence showed up at the theater that night, that's the place many of the *Hamilton* family were in, too, psychologically speaking. So, when Lin got word that the Vice-President elect would be there, he knew he couldn't let it pass without standing up and speaking, as always, with an eloquence few have ever been born with, for those who were afraid.

Lin was no longer performing in the show at that point, having moved on to other projects, so he, Tommy Kail and Jeffrey Seller crafted a message to be read by the actor playing Hamilton, Brandon Dixen, directly to Pence from the stage during the curtain call. Here's what it said:

> *Thank you so much for joining us tonight. You know, we had a guest in the audience this evening. And Vice President-elect Pence, I see you're walking out but I hope you will hear us just a few more moments. There's nothing to boo here ladies and gentlemen. There's nothing to boo here, we're all here sharing a story of love.*
>
> *We have a message for you, sir. We hope that you will hear us out. And I encourage everybody to pull out your phones and tweet and post because this message needs to be spread far and wide, OK?*
>
> *Vice President-elect Pence, we welcome you and we truly thank you for joining us here at* Hamilton: An American Musical, *we really do. We, sir, we are the diverse America who are alarmed and anxious that your new administration will not protect us—our planet, our children, our parents— or defend us and uphold our inalienable rights, sir. But we truly hope that this show has inspired you to uphold our American values and to work on behalf of all of us.*
>
> *All of us.*
>
> *Again, we truly thank you for sharing this show. This wonderful American story told by a diverse group of men and women of different colors, creeds, and orientations.*

When Brandon began, I started a live video, and to my astonishment, it had soon been watched by over one hundred thousand people. *Hamilton* had suddenly and quite unexpectedly become a notable face to the resistance to the president-elect's positions.

Not long after the message was read to unbridled ovation and many tears, Mike Pence left the theater, and controversy entered. Upon getting wind of what had transpired, the president-elect had this to say on his communication platform of choice, Twitter:

"The Theater must always be a safe and special place. The cast of Hamilton *was very rude last night to a very good man, Mike Pence. Apologize!"*

And that opened the flood gates.

Anyone who was in the theater that night can tell you that "rudeness" was absolutely not the intention, nor, from the perspective of most, the result. It was simply a worried people, peacefully airing their concerns to the new powers that be. But some of Trump's supporters certainly did not see it that way, as I learned firsthand the following morning. The information office at the Rodgers, located right across from mine, and within earshot of one side of phone conversations, was inundated with calls and messages from those who were unhappy with the previous night's display of First Amendment Rights. While we readied for the Saturday matinee performance, I listened as angry voicemails, some frightening in nature, continued to play. And it wasn't just phone calls—when I left to get dinner in between shows, in front of the theater police were setting up barricades for an expected demonstration later that evening.

Hamilton was also receiving a great deal of encouragement, though, and as supporters of the president-elect gathered in protest outside, a welcome ally arrived that night in the person of Bruce Springsteen.

He asked me what it had been like the night before. After telling him about the most electrifying experience I'd ever had in a theater, The Boss said, "That must have been something."

Once Springsteen had taken his seat, and the show had begun, I could hear the group of protesters stationed on the sidewalk just beyond the lobby doors, chanting something. I gingerly stepped outside, momentarily taken aback by the number of people, and the anger with which they shouted, having become one organism, believing one thing – they were right and I, the guy approaching them who'd come from inside wearing the word "Hamilton" on his chest, was not.

★

November 22, 2016

I just had a pretty cool experience. Trump supporters are outside the theater. They are protesting and yelling, "Apologize to Pence." I walked right up to the front line. I had my *Hamilton* shirt on so, as I got closer, they got louder, and were eventually screaming right in my face. I leaned in to one of the men and softly asked, "Can we talk for a minute?" To my surprise, he stopped shouting and said, "Um . . . sure." So, over the loud chanting, we talked. I asked him what was most upsetting to him. He answered. And I responded. About a minute into our conversation, I realized the rest of the shouting had stopped. And the crowd was listening to this gentleman and I, sometimes adding their own thoughts to the back and forth. By the end, I was shaking a woman's hand as she said, "Thank you for taking the time to hear me out. In the end, we're all Americans."

We are.

And, beyond that, we're all people. Every one of us, stuffed with our fears and desires and hopes and thoughts and dreams. And we're in this thing together. It's the only way we're going to make it. When you see someone shouting, realize there's a reason. And do what you can to understand that reason, regardless of whether or not you agree. You may just end up shaking their hand.

And, after that, it's a whole lot easier to reach their heart.

I posted that, and believed it. However, I knew the next years would be personally challenging. There's always a period of adjustment, of course, from administration to administration, while the country eases into the new directions we've chosen. But it felt to me as though there wouldn't be much ease, in this case, as we abruptly and starkly shifted course.

Springsteen told me in the Rodgers lobby how unsettled he was by the new path we'd chosen, and how much he would miss Obama. He'd openly supported Barack, playing some of his campaign rallies in 2012, and even giving a private concert at the White House to thank him at the end of his two terms. To close out that East Room send-off, the final song he played was "In the Land of Hopes and Dreams," containing the following lyrics:

> *Grab your ticket and your suitcase*
> *Thunder's rolling down this track*
> *Well you don't know where you're going now*
> *But you know you won't be back*
> *Well darling, if you're weary*
> *Lay your head upon my chest*
> *And I'll stand by your side*
> *You'll need a good companion now*
> *For this part of the ride*
> *And leave behind your sorrows*
> *Let this day be the last*
> *Well tomorrow there'll be sunshine*

And all this darkness past
Well big wheels roll through fields where sunshine streams
Oh meet me in the land of hope and dreams

A few weeks later, Obama gave his farewell address in Chicago. He tried, in it, to quell our fears, much like Washington had. Knowing how distraught his supporters, in particular, were, he wanted to let us know he'd still be with us, "in the midst of his fellow-citizens," still around to help us through the uncertain times. Not coincidentally, it was the same Springsteen anthem from above that played Obama off the stage after he'd finished. It's a song that says we're all in this together, "saints and sinners," "kings and fools," lost souls and the broken-hearted. All of us. It's a song of hope, a song about heading through darkness, all together, to a place where "sunshine streams." So it made complete sense to have that song blast from the stadium-sized speakers after Obama concluded his speech like this:

> *In his own farewell address, George Washington wrote that self-government is the underpinning of our safety, prosperity, and liberty, but "from different causes and from different quarters much pains will be taken . . . to weaken in your minds the conviction of this truth." And so we have to preserve this truth with "jealous anxiety;" that we should reject "the first dawning of every attempt to alienate any portion of our country from the rest or to enfeeble the sacred ties" that make us one . . .*
>
> *It falls to each of us to be those anxious, jealous guardians of our democracy; to embrace the joyous task we've been given to continually try to improve this great nation of ours. Because for all our outward differences, we, in fact, all share the same proud title, the most important office in a democracy: Citizen. Citizen . . .*
>
> *My fellow Americans, it has been the honor of my life to serve you. I won't stop. In fact, I will be right there with you, as a citizen, for all my remaining days. But for now, whether you are young or whether you're young at heart, I do have one final ask of you as your President—I'm asking you to believe. Not in my ability to bring about change—but in yours.*
>
> *I am asking you to hold fast to that faith written into our founding documents; that idea whispered by slaves and abolitionists; that spirit sung by*

immigrants and homesteaders and those who marched for justice; that creed reaffirmed by those who planted flags from foreign battlefields to the surface of the moon; a creed at the core of every American whose story is not yet written: Yes, we can.

We were going from a president who spoke in these inspiring, hopeful, inclusive ways, his parting remarks so squarely and comfortably seated in a lineage begun by the exalted farewell address of George Washington, revealing him a natural, though generations hence successor to that sort of high oratory, to someone who said . . . things much more difficult to imagine on White House stationary, or printed in future history textbooks meant to be read by young students: "As the 45th President of the United States once noted, 'Sorry losers, but my I.Q. is one of the highest—and you all know it!'"

It was all surreal. While in real life, the one being shouted at us with every headline, where the foundations of American democracy seemed to be threatened, on the stage the unlikely story of the founding of that democracy was playing out in the biggest hit in Broadway's history. And playing out in a way that sought to highlight what has been lacking since that founding, the irony of ironies in the land of "All men are created equal." A show about the founding of America by immigrants, using mostly minority actors to tell the story, "America *then* being portrayed by America *now*," as *Hamilton* director Tommy Kail said, just happened to become a part of our popular culture right at the time a president-elect was trying to stoke fears about immigrants, painting "them" in broad, frightening strokes. "They" who had founded the system he now sat atop. What were the chances this should pop onto the scene, right then?

Hamilton, arriving on the cosmic stage precisely when it did, a time when its depicted democracy felt as though it was being challenged in ways it hadn't in many, many years, is one of the things that makes me wonder if there isn't some vast orchestrator pulling galactic strings. If, somewhere, a mind as great as Lin's, but with larger pens, writes not on paper but on the still-to-us-mysterious canvas of creation, "And now, enter this . . . and then, just when they need it, just when the fear rises in them to a pitch fevered and desperate, as the way gets ever more shrouded in uncertainty, enter . . . this."

As we struggled to come to terms with what to do next, how to begin the long slog through the next four years, *Hamilton* became a rallying spot for many. A place where hope still shone. The "great unfinished symphony" that is America remains so, and we're bound to have some discordant notes along the way. *Hamilton* was helping some (me) to believe we were not now forever headed in a direction marked by fear and division. I knew, watching the show every night, that when the right people rise up, with the right motives and the right words, the melody can quickly emerge from the din, and voice by voice the harmony again finds its footing. Though the great symphony might have felt far off right then, *Hamilton* was helping people hear the tune. And, to me, there was something very familiar about that.

I'd been this unsure before. More so, even. As a child, *nothing* made sense to me. The world seemed entirely too big for a human-sized brain, or at least a my-sized brain, and the confusion the questions left me with was overwhelming. What to do with existence, how to use it and where to go with it, was just too much for a kid to ponder, I thought, and as I stared into the deep and unending night, and a frighteningly nebulous future, I wondered if I'd ever not be afraid. If I'd be brave enough to keep searching.

And then, one day as a still scared teenager, I walked into an auditorium.

As I began to get messages from hundreds of people following the posts I'd written about what happened at *Hamilton*, almost all of them looking for hope, almost all of them feeling battered by a stormy and uncertain sea, I had the distinct feeling that *Hamilton* was going to be a beacon, pointing to, and even bringing, brighter days.

After all, this was not the first time theater had lit my way.

ACT 2, SCENE 3

(NOT) REDEFINING BRAVERY

"Once I spoke the language of the flowers,
Once I understood each word the caterpillar said,
Once I smiled in secret at the gossip of the starlings,
And shared a conversation with the housefly
in my bed.
Once I heard and answered all the questions
of the crickets,
And joined the crying of each falling dying
flake of snow,
Once I spoke the language of the flowers. . . .
How did it go?
How did it go?"

—SHEL SILVERSTEIN
WHERE THE SIDEWALK ENDS

There is only one moment in my life that I have been truly brave.

See, I'm afraid of, well . . . pretty much everything. Spiders, for instance. And elevators. And heights. And being trapped in an elevator on a high floor with a spider inside.

Also, needles (I fainted once during a routine blood draw), and tight spaces (I actually just fainted again reading back the sentence about the blood draw), and biting into an apple to find a worm (or, worse, half a worm), and marriage and being single and flying and all the regular stuff, too, like snakes, cows, and tornados.

So, when I tell you about my bravest moment, I'll not be bragging (I'm also afraid of sounding like I'm bragging). It's my one brave moment amongst a sea of wide-ranging cowardice.

But, it *was* brave. Even looking back on it, I wonder from where the courage came.

There was a man who was well known to be something of a monster. Not something of—he *was* a monster. More powerful than I and most, cruel and terrible in every way, he struck fear into the heart of anyone he looked upon. No one dared cross him, imagining the wrath he'd bring down upon them and their families, falling instead in lock-step behind him, finding it far easier to join his band of evil-makers than to get in the way. But one day, for some reason, some impenetrable reason, I got in the way. Specifically, I got in *his* way. His name, difficult even now to type, was . . . Gus Butterfield. Gus. Butterfield. The roughest, toughest, baddest dude in all the known land.

And he was four feet tall.

He was like three-and-a-half to four feet tall.

And all three-and-a-half to four feet of him stuffed so full of menace, he oozed awful at the seams.

Let me paint you a picture. Let's say, hypothetically, you'd always been a quiet kid. For as long as you could remember, you'd spent your time mostly on the inside—not of your house, but of you. You wondered a lot about where all of this came from, including you. Life, to you, seemed so big and baffling and breathtaking a thing, that you assumed everyone else was in the same position. All perpetually awe struck. We were all the Goonies, you thought. All of us together on this adventure, sailing every day farther into the mystery, reaching out and pulling together bits and pieces of the puzzle as we went. We were all the Goonies, and life itself was One-Eyed Willy . . . something big and forbidding, but ultimately, there to teach us something—knowledge being the treasure awaiting the valiant who took the trip.

Then let's say, hypothetically, you were overjoyed when your very first day of school came around, and looking very much forward to the idea that you were finally going to get some answers. Together, you and your classmates would begin to unravel this thing. Sure, you were *incredibly* nervous about leaving your parents for an entire day to be with strangers, but you were trying your three-and-a-half feet of damndest to focus, hypothetically, on the fun you were going to have as you started to figure some stuff out!

And then you peed your pants.

Hypo-wet-ically.

(I'm sorry. I really couldn't help it. I tried, but, like the kid in this story, I couldn't help it).

Friends, there are some things you should try to avoid doing on your first day of school, if at all possible. We don't have space here to get into all of them, so I'll just give you the main one; folks, don't pee your pants on the first day of first grade. Because if you do, everyone will know it. I mean, I don't know how, but they will know even before the event is over. There must be some kind of as yet undiscovered neural communication network evolution has devised that allows children to get together very quickly on figuring out the hierarchy. Obviously, if a kid pees his or her pants, he or she is not the fittest. And you know how survival works. If there is someone lower than you on the food chain, that's good for you.

The more people below you the better, but the main thing is just not to be the lowest. So, if a weakness is sensed on the first day of first grade, a primordial instinct is activated.

And they'll pounce.

Imagine you had been outside at recess playing a game where your whole class was holding hands in a circle. You really had to go to the bathroom, but so shy were you, that you were afraid to speak up in front of everyone (I mean, in this story, you're a kid who really is afraid of *everything*—even asking to use the bathroom). And, eventually, you just couldn't hold it anymore.

As the wet mark spread, so did the laughs, and Mrs. Brown, let's call her, finally noticed. With some pointing and jeering, you were brought inside to the office to call your mom.

When she arrived with a fresh change of clothes, she oh so gently took you by the hand, and led you to the bathroom (which, in this story we're making up on the spot as an illustration, is cruelly located right at the back of the classroom). Your face burned with shame as you walked past your schoolmates to get there. Once inside, you cried in her arms.

She got you cleaned up and changed while tears fell faster than she could dry them. You told her you didn't want to go back out there. "It's okay," she softly said. "It will be okay. This happens to everyone, sometimes. And, sometimes, you have to be brave."

She then smiled and joked, "And if any of those kids give you a problem, you just let me know, and they will be peeing their own pants by the time I'm done with them." She laughed when she said it, but somewhere you sensed she wasn't entirely kidding.

The bathroom door swung open and Mrs. Brown did her best to keep the class' attention on her. Your mom brought you to your seat, smiled, and kissed you on the head. Then, when a slight chuckle came from somewhere, she stood straight up and glared with a look that instantly transformed her into a lion.

You immediately knew you'd be safe behind that look for the rest of your life.

And, behind that look, the bravery she spoke of, small and trembling but there, was born.

She'll do such a good job that day that you'll have believed her. Everything *would* be okay.

But not yet.

Before everything would be okay, you'd have to go through a whole lot of, you know . . . crap. You'll be surprised to learn that not every kid is as caught up in the mystery of life as you are, and a lot of them have time for other things . . . like being cruel to each other.

And that'll confuse you.

Until that point, you grew up thinking everyone was good and on the same team. We were all alive, and trying to figure out together what that meant. Finding you were wrong about that might have thrown you.

It certainly did me. I'm not saying I'm the kid in this story (I am) but, like him, I did find myself befuddled. It wasn't only kids being unkind to each other at school. I'd come home and the news would be on. Stories of people doing far worse things to each other than what I'd witnessed on the playground met my eyes and ears. Things like war, where whole groups of strangers tried to kill other whole groups of strangers. It was something I simply couldn't grasp, and the lack of acceptable answers from my parents or catechism teacher or priest was frightening to me.

Eventually, in fourth grade, we moved out of that town and into a new one. Though the kids at my "fresh start" school weren't aware of my pee-checkered past, it sure felt like they were. This new group of schoolmates struck me as just as cruel and unaware of how enormous a riddle life is as the kids I'd thankfully left behind, eager for a new beginning. But instead, things just picked back up where they had left off, it seemed—same bullies, different faces.

And it really made me start to wonder. See, in the Goonies, they eventually realized the only way to solve the mystery, the only way to indeed *survive*, was to do it together. If life really was a Goonies type scenario, it seemed to me we were well past the part of the story where we come to understand that and start making our way to the happy ending. *Was I wrong?* I wondered. *Had I been feeling a meaning to life that wasn't there? Could it be that this was all the result of chance? Was it possible that life just happened by luck* (or lack thereof, depending on your perspective—and how many times you've peed your pants at school)? *Was it just a bunch of particles bumping into each other until* we *happened, and that we would live and grow old and die and it would all amount to a cold and senseless nothing?*

I decided I'd take my question right to the top.

My family wasn't a very religious one. I'd been baptized and was going to make my first communion and all that, and we went to church maybe on

Christmas and Easter, but that was the extent of it. I asked my mom and dad if they believed in God, and they both said, "Yes," and since they seemed like pretty smart people, I supposed they must be right. But beyond this vague understanding of a guy in the clouds who sometimes went bowling and in doing so made thunder, so many questions remained. It was suggested by my catechism teacher that I might find some of the answers I was looking for in the Bible.

The Bible, she said, was "the word of God," and the ultimate truth.

Well great! I thought. *Why hadn't someone given me this inside information sooner? I'd been asking all of these tough questions that no one had been adequately answering, while the ultimate truth was waiting for me right inside a readily available book!*

The Bible is a two-parter, I discovered, and I decided to start at the beginning with the "Old Testament." Obviously. You wouldn't watch the sequel before the original. You'd surely be confused if you did it that way. But reading the Old Testament, I was utterly baffled. It was really crazy. There was stuff in there like this: "If a pit is opened or dug and left uncovered, and an animal falls into it, the owner of the pit shall pay the owner of the animal but he can keep the dead animal."

Umm . . . what? You mean to tell me that just after throwing the rings around Saturn, God was like, "You know what, I'd better go back and give them some very detailed advice on what to do if a cow falls in a hole. Otherwise, a cow is going to fall into a hole, and everyone is just going to stand around scratching their heads."

There's also lots of stuff about what you can stone people to death for, and how to cut your hair.

At that young age, it just didn't make any sense to me. These were not the answers I was looking for. The God of this book didn't fit, in my mind, with the pictures of space I'd seen in school or while visiting the Smithsonian Institute on a field trip. The universe seemed far too grand to me to be created by the same something that said, "When fighting another man, chop off his wife's hand if she grabs your genitals."

But, if my mom and dad were right, and there is a God, and she/he/it or whatever created this mess—from my fourth-grade perspective, I saw it as a mess—there must be a reason it is the way it is. Why would God allow all the pain I saw if there wasn't a reason?

Considering that the Bible wasn't helping me the way I'd hoped it would, perhaps confusing me even further, in fact, I decided to make a deal with she or he or it or whatever. I had taken to looking at the night sky quite a lot. Not finding answers down here, I wondered if there might be any up there. So, late one summer evening, I went outside and laid down on our front lawn. It was a perfectly clear night, a billion stars sparkling over the small stretch of the firmament that I could see between our tall trees. "Okay, God," I began, "if you're really there, I have some questions. Not about whether or not you can boil a baby goat in her mother's milk. I *was* wondering about that, but luckily that one you answered in the book. I have other questions. And I know lots of people must ask you this stuff, and for whatever reason you don't or can't answer. So, here's the deal—if you can give me a sign, right now, that you are there, something I will *know* is a sign, I'll accept that there are things I just can't know right now. I'll be fine with that. But I have to know that there's a reason for all of this. I have to know, if all of this pain is around, that it means something. I'll be able to let go of needing answers if I can just know you're there. If you can give me a sign . . . right . . . NOW."

And at that moment, over my head, a shooting star tore through the atmosphere.

I mean, it *tore* through. I actually heard it sizzle past.

The area that I could see above was not that large. We had tall trees on all sides, so it was really just directly overhead that was visible. And in that little patch of sky, a great expanse of faith opened up within me. It made me believe, in that moment, that though I didn't understand anything, it all meant something.

That's a true story.

So powerful a moment was it, that it has informed my entire life, and I still call on the memory whenever I need a boost after watching the news.

Could it have been coincidence? Of course. The more rational among us will certainly see it as such. And I understand. But my irrationality helped me survive my incessant questioning—and Gus Butterfield.

Of all the questions I had for God, Gus was the biggest, with regard to my immediate life in fourth grade. I couldn't guess the reason an all powerful entity would create something seemingly designed specifically to torment. Since it did, though, every day I'd wake up and psychologically suit up for battle. Gus wouldn't allow an opportunity pass to go out of his way to make fun of me in some way, and other kids who were happy to not be on the bottom would do the same.

Far from being his only target, one day, I saw Gus on the playground picking on someone else. His name was Chris Everite, and he was one of the nice ones. He and I didn't really speak, both being on the introverted side, but we took Karate together once a week after school.

When I say I "took Karate," what I mean is I showed up at a class where a teacher yelled at us for two hours, striking me funny any time I thought, *We are paying for this?*

I didn't take karate so much as survive karate, but Chris was good at it. He was a much more advanced belt than me (not a high bar, being I was at the first belt) and compared to me, he might as well have been a ninja. So, when I came across Gus and Chris in the playground that day, I thought, *Well, Gus doesn't know who he is messing with this time.*

I found out later from Chris exactly what had happened; Gus had taken Chris' ball. Chris politely asked for it back, but Gus, seemingly made to lead little children out to midnight lawns to question God about what he was doing, refused to give it. Chris turned away, resigned to surrendering his ball, and whispered under his breath, "Asshole."

But it wasn't under his breath enough.

Gus heard it, and by the time I arrived, he had Chris backed up against a tree with what seemed like the entire fourth and fifth grade classes standing behind him, begging for him to remind Chris who was boss. It was brutal to watch. Chris literally had his back to this tree with nowhere left to escape, while Gus sadistically repeated, "Call me an asshole again. Do it. Call me an asshole again. Call me an asshole! DO IT!"

Knowing Chris was a green belt, I wondered why he didn't show Gus his ninja stuff. Instead, he just stood there and took it, looking at the ground. I was the only person standing behind Chris, so I couldn't see his face. When I moved a bit closer and to his side, I was shocked to find that he was crying.

And something came over me.

It was one thing for Gus to pick on me, but seeing him do it to this other kid, to the point of drawing tears . . . I lost my prudent mind for a moment.

"You're an asshole!" I yelled.

As if I had no control, suddenly, of my vocal apparatus, those words slipped out of my mouth. I didn't have command of my eyes, either, it didn't seem, because they just stared straight into Gus'. The two classes worth of students behind Gus suddenly became silent, shocked at this utterly unanticipated turn of events. With bated breath they waited for what would happen next. Surely this new kid would be beaten to a pulp. In my own mind, in fact, I wondered in the awful, expectant pause if my sister would knock down the wall between our rooms to make herself a master suite, now that I'd be gone.

But that didn't happen. To my very great relief, a relief the depth of which I can't properly convey, Gus just said something pithy. "Whatever," I think it was.

And he walked away.

Most people are afraid, I think. Even Gus Butterfield. Perhaps especially Gus Butterfield. We just hide it with varying degrees of success.

Life went on, and as it turned out, Gus was far from the only bully I'd encounter (in fact, I'd one day realize we sometimes elect them president). However, after that very public moment, things were easier for me. I wouldn't find "my tribe" until high school, but it wasn't quite the hell it had been before.

And though I still couldn't fathom what it was all about, I'd gotten my sign, and deep inside I did feel that it all had a purpose. Now I just needed to sort out my corner of the purpose.

WHAT TO SAY TO YOU?

"Have patience with everything that remains unresolved in your heart. Try to love the questions themselves, like locked rooms and like books written in a foreign language. Do not now look for the answers. They cannot now be given to you because you could not live them. It is a question of experiencing everything. At present you need to live the question. Perhaps you will gradually, without even noticing it, find yourself experiencing the answer, some distant day."

—RAINER MARIA RILKE
LETTERS TO A YOUNG POET

I left Gus and the past on the playground that day in fourth grade after our confrontation, and walked back into the school intent on finding my place in the universe. But that would be a goal much easier set than achieved. I mean, what in the world is a person supposed to do with something so precious as a life? After all, "You only live once," as I was far too often reminded. YOLO is now a thing. It's on bumper stickers and T-shirts and the lips of many a dorm room philosopher. It's meant as a light-hearted way of saying, "Hey, you might as well go for it!" But for me the words "You only live once" wrapped around my psyche like an anvil necklace.

"Once? Once? You have got to be kidding me," my ten-year-old self said to the God he imagined sent him that meteorite. "In an apparently infinite universe, with an uncountable number of choices to be made (most of which will probably be mistakes, if life so far is any indication—do you remember the time I thought it might be nice to paint our rabbit a new color?) You only get one shot at this thing? One? That's a lot of pressure, man! Come on! What if Mario only had one shot? No one would ever reach the last flag, that's what. The end of the game would forever remain a mystery. If Zelda couldn't start over after missteps, well, no one would ever have defeated Ganon. Do you have any idea how many lives it took me to get safely across the road in Frogger for the first time?"

God didn't answer me. Not in any way I could hear, anyway. Somewhere in the back of my mind, though, I felt like (and hoped) the philosophers and our priest might be wrong, that maybe we did live more than once. It just made more sense to me. But I didn't want to bank on that, and just in case YOLO really was the way of things, and we did get just one chance, then I'd better be careful about what I did with it. Most of the kids I went to school with seemed to already have a solid grasp on how they wanted to use their one life.

But I simply had no idea.

So, I started to ask around. And the answer came easily and unanimously; "You can be whatever you want."

That's what everyone said.

My mom said it, my grandma said it, my teachers said it—even our very nice mail-person said it to me once (as I sincerely wondered why, out of all the things he could be, he chose mail-person? *Maybe it's the cool jeep he gets to drive with the steering wheel on the wrong side? Or the shorts?* My four-year-old mind postulated).

Well, awesome, I thought. *Anything I want to be, I can be!*

As cool as the jeep with the wheel on the wrong side was, I didn't want to be a mailperson, I didn't think (I have an irrational fear of paper cuts). My mom was a nurse, and there was no way I wanted to do that. She would regale us with stories of the emergency room—a motorcycle accident that left a leg hanging just by the skin, the nauseating smell from a man's feet that hadn't been washed in years undergoing emergency surgery, and the time a crazed man, high on something (not life, I guessed), was wheeled in after being found holding his you-know-what in a Ziplock bag, which he'd just cut off with a razor blade because he was afraid of sexually transmitted diseases.

These stories invariably left me weak in the knees. I did not have the constitution to be a nurse.

My stepfather was a carpenter. He owned a small construction company, and my cousin and I spent the summers of my childhood helping him "build houses," which meant doing all the jobs no one who owned a company would want to do themselves—we dug holes, mixed cement, moved endless piles of wood that confoundingly never got smaller, and filled dumpster upon dumpster with stuff we most likely shouldn't have been touching with bare hands (does anyone know what asbestos looks like?).

I did that job all through college, but I knew on day one that if I could "do anything I want," there surely must be something I want to do more than carry fifty-pound bags of asphalt shingles up a ladder to a roof every day.

Mostly, what I wanted to do was just have a good time. To enjoy myself. I wanted life to be an uninterrupted party surrounded by friends and loved ones, where we always feel the way I do after precisely a glass and a half of White Zinfandel (which is, hands down, the best wine).

I wanted to spend a lifetime having fun. As Dudley Moore rhetorically asked in Arthur (my favorite movie as a child—like I've said, I was a weird kid), "Isn't fun the best thing to have?"

So, what job offered that? Unlike a lot of my classmates who had some notion of what they wanted to be when they "grew up," no clear sense had emerged for me. I *said* all the "normal" little kid things—"I want to be a fireman," while in my little kid head I was thinking, *No freaking way. Fire is scary. And very hot.* I couldn't imagine spending my life sweaty and afraid.

"I want to be an astronaut." Sure, the view seems to be stirring at a soul level. "Looking into the eyes of God," type of stuff. Every person that returns from space is changed. Seeing our home hanging in space is a perspective most will never have, but one that would, could we all simultaneously experience it, change us and how we treat each other and the planet overnight. But where in "the world" does an astronaut poop?

Baseball player. I loved playing baseball. And here's where the "you can do anything you want" thing was first put to the test for me. At thirteen, I was on the traveling All Star Team. We were in the tournament that ends up in Williamstown for the Little League World Series. A big deal (it seemed back then). In the bottom of the seventh inning, we were up by a few runs when our pitcher got hurt. I was the last available pitcher on the roster, so I was brought in from shortstop to take over. All I had to do was get three outs, and we'd be moving on in the state tournament. Thousands sat in the stands (I think it was probably like seventy-five people, but at the time I was sure it was thousands) including my poor mother. What I *wanted* to do was strikeout three people in a row with the most powerful fastball anyone had ever seen come from a thirteen-year-old arm, and go home victorious. But what I *did* was walk about ten people, hit two or three batters with errant pitches along the interminable way, and leave us, when the dust had finally, mercifully settled, down by approximately twelve runs. I know this story strains credibility, and I've already admitted to exaggeration before with the size of the crowd, but this part, a largely faded memory, hasn't altered or embellished—I walked people for about an hour. If there had been anyone sitting in the stands who didn't really understand baseball before that game, they must have been utterly mystified by what they were watching now.

The inning, I was sure, was never going to end. Come to think of it, I don't remember it ending. It may still be going on. So, the old "you can do anything you want" seemed to have some caveats. You can do anything you want if you can do the thing you want to do. That seemed a bit closer to the truth. You could be a professional, Major League baseball player if you had world-class baseball skills. If you are barely coordinated enough to walk across an empty room without finding something to knock into, you may have some trouble getting the MLB scouts to notice you—for the right reasons, anyway.

So, my dream of playing for The Red Sox seemed to be out.

ACT 2, SCENE 5

SOMETHING NEW INSIDE

"The earth keeps some vibration going
There in your heart, and that is you.
And if the people find you can fiddle,
Why, fiddle you must, for all your life."

—EDGAR LEE MASTERS
SPOON RIVER ANTHOLOGY

By the time I reached high school, my social anxiety had not abated. When, in my freshman year, we had to give a presentation for an English class on Shakespeare, I didn't sleep for the whole week leading up to it, and thought the Bard quite the frothy flap mouthed mumble-news for the torment he'd been putting kids like me through for a few hundred years.

Then, one day, in my "will-things-ever-be-easier?" sophomore year, the theater department was holding auditions for the student-written, one-act plays. Obviously, that was not something I would do. I recalled, though, going to see the student plays the year before as a freshman.

Sitting small and quiet in the back row of the auditorium (even that I did shyly), I watched in awe and envy as a guy named Mike Something-Or-Other performed a comic scene with another student actor. As the audience wailed in laughter, I sat motionless. It wasn't that I didn't think it was funny—I most certainly did. My quiet came from the feeling that comedy was something special. Sitting in the dark, all those people laughing not at each other, but *with* each other, was magic. What was more, I found I knew where the funny was. I could feel it. I thought, *Oh, if he does this next, it'll bring the house down.* I wished with everything I had that this type of courage resided within me. The courage to share your heart, and make people laugh with it.

But that wasn't a mettle I possessed.

So, the following year, when signs went up announcing auditions, no matter how deeply I wished I had it in me to try, I knew I would not be attending.

However, my "girlfriend" did have it in her to try (girlfriend is in quotes because what I mean is we'd held hands this one time on a Ferris wheel at the town fair—which made me sweat uncontrollably. Other kids were already, you know, "doing it"—or, so they said—and I just couldn't grasp it. Just the hand-holding was making me schvitz). I decided to go along with my "girlfriend" to her audition and offer moral moist-palmed support.

Watching from the back of the theater as classmate after classmate got up so easily in front of all these people to read a scene, I found myself nervous just thinking about it. I simply couldn't fathom how they made themselves do it. Please then, consider my utter shock when my name got called to audition. Unbeknownst to me, a friend who knew quite well my fear of standing up in front of people, let alone talking in front of them, had filled out an audition form in my name as a joke. All eyes turned—I mean heads positively jerked around with alarming, whiplash-inducing speeds to look at me. So, I got up, picked up the paper with the scene on it, and rubber-legged my way up onto the stage. I'd been watching the auditions for a while, so I knew the scene. Sitting alone in the back, I'd been thinking, *I wish they would do it this way. They are missing the laugh there and there.* My partner spoke his line, and somehow, I managed to speak mine. I gripped the paper and stared only at it, watching as a bead of sweat fell from my forehead and onto the sheet, blurring a word. Halfway down the page, we got to the line where they hadn't been doing it the way my brain heard and saw it. I took a minuscule pause (up to that point I couldn't get the words out fast enough, knowing that once they'd all been spoken, I could recede back into anonymity) and suddenly I became present—and said the line my way. A harrowing split second of terrible quiet passed, before out in the house a sound came that changed my life—it was laughter—laughter not *at* me, but *with* me. And I was hooked.

Finding theater was like a life raft suddenly and unexpectedly falling around me after being so long lost at sea. Through a spur-of-the-moment prank that would touch every moment after, I'd found the Goonies I'd once imagined we all were. The "theater kids" were interested in knowing about life. Our director, Pat, would, in fact, teach us that acting is *entirely* about looking at things from many different angles and perspectives. In order to be a good actor, you need to be full of empathy, and deeply wonder what it's like to be someone else. The people I found myself in rehearsals with, after getting cast in a small role following that first audition, realized life *itself* was extraordinary, and that its simple existence required our full attention.

Theater kids were the ones I'd been searching for.

Theater people, I immediately knew, were my kind of people.

From the moment I stepped on stage, and that laugh leapt out from the darkness, I knew the stage was the safest place I'd ever be. I still felt utterly lost with regard to how we'd all gotten here, and where it was all heading, but finally, I wasn't lost alone.

And that is the difference between night and day, pals.

So, theater it was. I studied it in college, then went to grad school for it—just because I wanted to be sure and start my stage acting career—careers which are so commonly highly lucrative—with at least something of a fiscal challenge. As David Mamet, the Pulitzer Prize-winning playwright, told me after I'd gone to grad school and gathered a substantial amount of debt doing so, "You don't need to go to school for acting. If anything, if you come out of school a better actor, it's in spite of the 'training' you got."

"Oh," I said.

So, I moved to New York, and just as I imagined, have spent the past twelve years on Broadway.

Selling over-priced Junior Mints.

I did some acting work here and there, and loved it. However, it wasn't nearly enough to pay my big city rent. So, as most artists do, I took a "day job." I thought working as a bartender for Broadway shows would, in fact, be the *perfect* "day job" for an actor, and one I'd keep for a year or so, just until I "made it."

But here I was, a full decade later, more than ten years after meeting the Cup Guy, still handing out those cups. While, just feet away, young men and women were living the dream I'd so long held in my heart. This is where the sadness was coming from on the day we had the softball team Ham4Ham. To daily be that close to *Hamilton* was simultaneously thrilling, and heart-breaking.

And the heartbreak wasn't just because these people on stage were experiencing the thing I'd always hoped for—it was also the realization that I didn't have what it takes to do what they do. I don't have the incredible physical prowess and rhythmic acumen to perform the *Hamilton* choreography, and I wasn't born with the voice my brain always imagined I had been and my shower walls helped me hear. I was an okay actor (despite my actor training) but was, without question, not Broadway material.

This was a tough truth to face, and I was staring directly at it. Every new actor that stepped into a role and hit notes that my body simply won't, and moved in ways my DNA doesn't seem to contain the instructions for, confirmed what I suspected that day on the mound: *You can't necessarily be whatever you want.*

But you can keep finding things you want to be.

And that might be the most important saving grace the God my shooting star gave me baked into the universe.

ACT 2, SCENE 6

LOOK AROUND, LOOK AROUND

"There is a time in every man's education when he arrives at the conviction that envy is ignorance; that imitation is suicide; that he must take himself, for better or worse, as his portion . . ."

—RALPH WALDO EMERSON
SELF-RELIANCE

Lin's Hamilton (and I think we can pretty safely say the real one, too) had great ambition. He worried enormously about his legacy and how history would speak of him.

That was something I related to. Again, given the possibility that this is our one chance at aliveness, our one opportunity to etch a story into the canvas of creation, I'd wanted to scrawl in letters so big and bold, to so thoroughly "suck the marrow out of life," to live in such a way that when I'd finished, I'd arrive at the end completely used up, having given everything and done it all, and done it so well they'd "tell my story," at least for a while. At least, maybe, when they'd talked about everything else, and had gotten to the uncomfortable place late in a brunch where any conversation is welcomed.

When it occurred to me, after realizing I do not possess the abilities to carry out, in the real world, what I saw in the inner place where hopes and dreams are born, that bartending was more likely my lot, that was tough. We can all understand that, of course. Hamilton would have understood, too.

The show named after him is so rich, that I'm struck in different ways by different things every time I watch it. And what started to stand out among the rest, lines that would cause me to raise my head from whatever I was doing every night and listen, was Eliza compelling Hamilton to see what it was he already had. He'd wanted to go off and fight in the war beside Washington, and lead a command so bravely that it'd be spoken of ever after. Eliza urges him to forget legacy, and as she caresses her pregnant belly, to notice what was in front of him. "Look around, look around at how lucky we are to be alive right now. Look around, look around. Look at where you are."

I found myself pausing every night to really take in the scene. Eliza's words pulled my attention from visions of what might have been, or what might be, and placed it on the here and now.

Rather than focusing on and feeling sad about not reaching the potential my high school self had imagined back when I was playing Nathan Detroit in Guys 'N Dolls, certain I was finding nuance in the character no one else had, nuance that would surely one day garner me the role in the Broadway revival (A revival in which, when it eventually did come to pass, they inexplicably cast Oliver Platt over me, as I discovered when tending bar there one week) I started, instead, to "get my Zen on," and simply . . . be.

When I looked around at where I was, well . . . how lucky was I? To be alive right now. Here. In this place. This bastion of life and hope, this oasis of beauty in a troubled time. I was seeing things every day that nearly brought me to tears, and often moved me well past "nearly." When I let go and opened my eyes to now, I became overwhelmed with gratitude. I was thankful to whatever does the putting that this is where I was put. For this current time, there was nowhere else, it now seemed, that I'd rather be. Where else, while things in the country felt to me as though they were careening off the rails, could I have been finding such hope? That lobby became a different world, one where goodness still reigned, and the hopefulness was often so consuming, overwrought people began to cry as soon as they entered. And that lobby started to feel more real than anything outside of it. I was having experiences every day that told me we were going to be okay.

I couldn't keep these joyful experiences to myself, so I began to share them with family and friends. And they didn't want to keep the stories either, so they also shared. We recognized that the things happening there in that lobby didn't belong to us. Others deserved to know about them, too. Because a kid crying due to their mighty love for *Hamilton*, moved to tears because they so value a story about overcoming odds together, and the power and primacy of love . . . well that's an antidote to anything that might be bringing you down.

Eliza says to Hamilton, "Let this chapter be the first moment, where you decide to stay. And I could be enough. And we could be enough. That would be enough."

I heard her. I understood her. This was more than enough. And as the stories about *that* enough further spread following the "Pence posts," something of a virtual support group grew up around the Rodgers' tales. My propensity to focus on what's right, rather than on what isn't yet, suddenly found a place, and with every message I received from a "stranger," I felt more useful than I ever had. I had thrown nothing away. I saw now that I'd been led inexorably to this spot, to be in this place, to see what I was seeing. Because that *Hamilton* sunshine is a powerful thing, and as the storm of the new presidency loomed always in the background, it parted clouds and helped some of us hang on.

It's my deep honor, now, to share some of that sunshine with you.

To be doing so in a book, I must say, comes as quite a surprise, because no matter how good of a scribe my mom thinks I am, writing one is something I hadn't envisioned. After all, she sees my wordsmithing skills in the same light that shone on my face for my grandmother, in which she saw a handsome so striking it rivaled young Marlon Brando. When I moved into the light of the real world, it seemed others didn't quite agree, placing my handsome not in the same category with even very old Marlon Brando.

The notion that I wouldn't be writing a book was bolstered further when I became not an author, but a professional seller of candy. I was, however, in Mr. Mikulack's "level one" English class in my freshman year of high school (much like Shakespeare was, I'm sure), and though I don't recall what a "dangling participle" is, I do remember the phrase. That ought to count for something . . . right? Yes, I was demoted to the "level two" class as a sophomore (which ended the parallels between Shakespeare and I—or "Shakespeare and me," depending on what that rule is, which is likewise lost to oblivion), but since, to my mom's delight, some roll of the celestial dice put me in a situation where a book just sort of . . . happened, for all you've read to this point I've drawn on all (the very little) I was able to summon from those halcyon days of grammatical erudition. (I, of course, thesaurused the heck out of that sentence).

But none of that was in mind when I'd sit on the train and tap out the following tales in the notes application on my phone, these immediate reactions to what I'd just experienced. The idea of them ending up in a book was the farthest thing from my thoughts. When I'd start each story, often beginning with the words, "Tonight, at *Hamilton* . . ." I was writing to my family and friends without concern for sentence structure or word choice, or what Mr. Mikulack would have said. They were meant to be brief, simple attempts at connection with those I love.

And, in that spirit, here they are, published largely as written.

ACT 3

THE STORY OF TONIGHT

"The universe is made of stories, not atoms."

—MURIEL RUKEYSER

---★---

November 23, 2016

Tonight at *Hamilton*, as I was bartending, a gentleman accidentally cut in front of a very, very large man in my line. The man who was cut silently mouthed the words "It's okay," to me from a good foot and-a-half over the line-cutter's head, telling me to go ahead and serve the person who'd somehow missed the near seven foot presence now standing behind him. The man who'd cut asked me for a drink, then looked over at someone being served by my fellow bartender in the other line, beginning this conversation with him:

> LINE-CUTTER: Hey, you must get this a lot, but you look a lot
>   like Mark Cuban. Know who that is?
> MARK CUBAN: *(smiling)* The name sounds familiar, yeah.
>   Enjoy the show.

As Mark walks away, I say to my customer, "When you're at *Hamilton*, if some-one reminds you of someone, it probably is the someone."

> LINE CUTTER: *(with genuine, extreme surprise)* Wait, that actu-
>   ally was Mark Cuban?!?
> ME: Yes. And you just cut in front of CC Sabathia.

At which the man turned around, looked up (way up) and judging by the look on his face, had the shock of his life, as a laughing CC clapped him on the shoulder.

---★---

December 3, 2016

"He could be funny anywhere. We were such close friends, he would come to all of our great family functions—weddings, bar mitzvahs, that kind of thing. He would sit with my older immigrant relatives, like he was one of the guys, and he would tell them about his journey from his little shtetl in Poland to America. One uncle of mine said, 'I came to America after World War Two, and I hitchhiked.' And Robin said, 'I waited until there was a 747 and a kosher meal.'"

—BILLY CRYSTAL

This is my friend Fran, and the plant she got me when I moved into my new place. Fran is the person who directs people towards the restrooms at the theatre. And it's serious business. If someone asks me where it is, I have to pretend like I don't know, somehow—"Gosh, they keep moving these things"—and suggest maybe they "Ask the woman over there."

You don't mess with Fran on this. That is what she is paid to do, and darn it, she will earn it. (On a side note, if you happen to be looking for the bathroom at the Richard Rodgers, chances are it's directly behind you).

During the run of *Hamilton*, Lin has become great friends with Fran.

But the best "show friend" she has made so far is Robin Williams.

When Robin made his Broadway debut at our theatre a few years ago, for reasons that become clear within moments of meeting her, he fell in love with Fran.

See, Fran is wickedly sharp and full of wit and wisdom. She's lived a life, and she has stories to share. She is funny and kind.

And . . . dirty.

She's also really dirty. When Fran calls me over and says, "Listen, I've got to tell you something," I know what is coming, and I blush before she even gets started. It's no mystery what Robin saw in Fran. She is an inspiration to me, and most everyone who meets her. She's living proof that you never have to stop having fun, or being engaged with life and people. Or being a little dirty, sometimes, too. After all, life gets dirty, and to really be in it, you've got to get some on you.

"When the game is over, I want that uniform to be a mess," my little league coach would say. I sense that Robin related to that. And talking to Fran is like sliding head first into second base. On a rainy day.

So, every night for months, Robin would sit with Fran in the lobby before the show. Just the two of them. He would listen to her stories, and laugh like crazy at her jokes. Like crazy. Every night. Usually, Robin made people feel better by being funny for them. But he must have felt Fran needed something else. So, he helped her sparkle by allowing her to be funny for him.

It wasn't all jokes, though. They had a lot of serious conversations, too. Quiet moments. Sad things sometimes, as well, Fran says (though she won't tell us what—it was between them).

When he wasn't manically zipping from character to character in his transcendent way, his never-to-be-witnessed-again way, he was just a guy. Just a sweetheart of a man. Who found great joy in the connection he'd made with the bathroom directions lady at the Richard Rodgers Theatre.

When the run of the show came to an end, Robin gave gifts to the house staff. Different things to different people. The play was about war, so he gave everyone dog tags. The house manager was given a bound script with a heartfelt note. He wanted to thank everyone for being a part of his experience, in whatever way they were. And all the ways were important to him.

See, "He was just the nicest man," as Fran says. She was sad, of course, about losing her friend. But it makes her happy to know that she was able to help him, if only for a time, muck up his uniform a little bit. Gone too soon, but my, what a game. I'm pretty sure God was satisfied with the state of Robin's jersey.

Fran is the only one who didn't get dog tags from Robin, by the way.

To her he gave a diamond necklace from Tiffany's.

Edit: Fran peacefully shuffled off this mortal coil this year, after 93 years full of laughter and love. It brings me great joy to imagine Robin standing there at the foot of her bed, guffawing before Fran even completes her first "other side" joke.

That I'm certain was just as blue as the ones she told before the wings.

Oh, Fran, how we'll miss ya. You did so much more than help people find the bathroom, that we'll all be lost for a while.

★

December 5, 2016

"We all start out knowing magic. We are born with whirlwinds, forest fires, and comets inside us. We are born able to sing to birds and read the clouds and see our destiny in grains of sand. But then we get the magic educated right out of our souls. We get it churched out, spanked out, washed out, and combed out. We get put on the straight and narrow and told to be responsible. Told to act our age. Told to grow up, for God's sake. And you know why we were told that? Because the people doing the telling were afraid of our wildness and youth, and because the magic we knew made them ashamed and sad of what they'd allowed to wither in themselves."

—ROBERT R. McCAMMON
BOY'S LIFE

For over a year, my coworker, Skyler, and I had been debating whether or not magic is real. My position has been that yes, indeed it is. Some of the things David Blaine does can only be explained by magic! *Actual* magic!

Of course, I know magic isn't real. I'm a very logical guy. It can all be elucidated with the study of mathematics, science, visual illusion, and copious practice. And yet, just for fun, I had continued to have this back and forth with Skyler, very frequently for months, any time we saw each other, even in passing, always revolving around David Blaine.

"There is no such thing as magic!" would be his constant refrain, while, "But, David Blaine!" would be mine.

Today, Skyler (who I very infrequently bartend with) and I stood behind a lonely bar at the Nederlander holiday party. Three bars were open, and we were working the one meant to pick up any stragglers on their way to the bathroom. Which meant we were alone the whole night.

Except for this moment when David Blaine came up the steps and walked over to us.

And, unprompted, before we could even say, "Hello," he said, "Want to see some magic?" as he pulled out a deck of cards.

111

He then proceeded to do a five-minute magic show for, literally, *just the two of us*. There was no audience but for these two people who'd been debating about him for over a year. Then, he turned around and went back downstairs (without using the bathroom—honestly, he didn't even use the bathroom! The only reason to come up those steps!)

I don't know if the (amazing) tricks he did are magic. But something, *something* extraordinary and unexplained is at work in the universe. And that something made both myself and my skeptical friend smile tonight, in absolute wonder.

I can't be certain about magic. But *wonder*, no doubt about it, is real. Even Skyler agrees with that.

P.S. To the right is the card I chose in my mind after David flashed a deck in front of me and said, "Pick one." I didn't physically pick one or point to anything, I just mentally had it in mind. A moment later, the card was no longer in the deck. It was folded up and hidden.

Under my watch. THAT I WAS WEARING. I asked him if he really is magical. He didn't answer. Which I take as a YES. (Of course, what's really magical here is my hair)

★

December 7, 2016

This week at *Hamilton* we had a "Make-A-Wish" kid. As you probably know, the Make-A-Wish Foundation is a charity that tries to grant a wish to a child fighting a particularly difficult medical battle. For this little girl, her wish was to see *Hamilton*. The show I "work" for every day.

It is so very easy to take it all for granted. And I don't just mean working somewhere a kid who may not survive wanted to go. We forget, daily, how amazing it *all* is. Every day we wake up and go to jobs and pay bills and don't notice that the universe is infinite. We forget, almost entirely, that we float through unending space on a tiny rock—an infinitesimally small piece of dust careening through the cosmos. And because we forget this miraculous thing, we find stuff to fill our time. Most of it is benign, and a lot of it is beautiful. But surprisingly, not all of it, because we also believe in and fight about and *kill* each other over divisions we've made up. Borders of one kind or another we've devised that so quickly lose meaning when viewed against the broader backdrop in which they exist. This notion has perhaps never been more clearly articulated than by Carl Sagan in 1990, after he saw this photo that Voyager 1 had just returned:

As the spacecraft left our solar system, from four billion miles away it turned its camera back toward home. Earth is just barely visible in the picture, a tiny speck in the light beam on the right, amidst a sea of emptiness. This first ever perspective inspired Sagan to write the following:

> *Think of the rivers of blood spilled by all those generals and emperors so that, in glory and triumph, they could become the momentary masters of a fraction of a dot. Think of the endless cruelties visited by the inhabitants of one corner of this pixel on the scarcely distinguishable inhabitants of some other corner, how frequent their misunderstandings, how eager they are to kill one another, how fervent their hatreds.*
>
> *There is perhaps no better demonstration of the folly of human conceits than this distant image of our tiny world. To me, it underscores our responsibility to deal more kindly with one another . . .*

To be alive appears to be a singular thing. In all our searching, as we've peered through the most powerful instruments humankind has conjured, we have discovered life in only one place. Just one speck in the vastness of space has been found to cradle material that has become aware. And that is here. On our dot.

It's just so easy, somehow, to lose sight of. And the forgetting leads to all sorts of things we wish it didn't—things we wouldn't possibly be able to do to each other if the lonely truth contained in this photo was held always in our minds, if we kept forefront the knowledge that most of it is impossibly cold and desolate and dark, and that for billons and billions of years and deeply empty miles one could travel, and not find awareness again.

If we were continuously conscious of this, we'd use our days only to wonder. If, with every morning, we reminded ourselves of the incomprehensible situation we find ourselves in, there would certainly be no time to hate. We'd not be able to look at another being of any "color" or "nationality" and see anything other than "fellow."

Fellow life. Fellow traveler. Fellow precious wonderer, drifting through space.

That kid, though.

That Make-A-Wish kid.

I sense she didn't need Voyager to get four billion miles away to know these things. I sense she required no photo to tell her how astounding a thing it is, that here, on a pale blue dot revolving through an average solar system situated on the outskirts of a galaxy in the midst of a limitless universe, some of that universe had come alive . . . and started to sing.

And so, what did she want to use her singular aliveness, knowing she may not possess it for all too long, doing?

Watching a musical.

Given the chance to do anything at all, that's how she chose to spend her precious awareness. Not hating or being afraid of or hurting "others" with her on the pale speck. To the contrary; she wanted to watch them sing and dance.

And the thought of her luminous, wisdom-filled eyes doing just that is my Voyager photo. She is my brilliant, shining dot.

December 8, 2016

Tonight at work, a young, very sweet man, with something akin to Down syndrome, came up to the bar and asked for a Reese's Pieces. He paid for it and said, "Thank you sir!" with a gigantic smile. He thought for a second, then asked, "Do you think I could get a Pepsi, too?" I answered, "Of course!" I handed him his drink and said, "That's eight dollars, please." He looked down at the bills he had crumpled up in his hands and counted them. When he realized he didn't have enough, the smile that hadn't left his face since he'd walked up suddenly fell. "Oh no. I'm so sorry. I don't think I have that." He felt so badly that I had already poured the soda that he asked if I could take back his candy, so he could pay for the drink. I told him not to worry, that I'd "buy" the soda for him. His eyes lit up like I had just handed him a thousand dollars. Or ten thousand. A million, even. It was a look of gratitude and awe taken to levels we seldom have the joy of seeing.

Just for a free soda.

"Oh wow! Thank you so much," he managed to squeeze from his stunned vocal cords as he walked away, smiling at me over his shoulder.

The next customer was an older gentleman who ordered a $12 cocktail. He handed me a twenty, then softly said, "You keep the rest." The person behind him was a young girl. She got her Pringles, and then asked if she could pay me for the young man's drink. I said her offer warmed my heart, but it was on me. She smiled, and left a five-dollar tip for her four-dollar candy.

Most of the time, it's a good world, friends.

More often than not, interactions between humans are marked by love. It may be subtle. You may not even be aware of it, but chances are, you are more loving than you realize. When you see someone crying, for instance, chances are, whether you know them or not, you have a wish (a wish that may stay secret even from yourself) that you could make the person feel better. And it's unfortunate that we don't notice that desire more often. Because that wish is the most accurate representation of who you truly are, once the muck of all the living has been rinsed away.

If you're anything like me, you probably get angry and yell and hurt people, even those you love, sometimes, and maybe have some pretty bad days.

But none of that, no matter how much there is, can erase the wish.

So, pay attention to that. Notice it.

Because the wish is you.

------------ ★ ------------

February 4, 2017

Tonight at *Hamilton* we had a gentleman whose name most people will not know. And yet, his contribution to basic goodness is titanic. When I think of what this now eighty-six-year-old man has seen, the unfairness and evil he has put his shoulders squarely into, bending with all his might that "moral arch" toward justice, I'm astounded.

Looking into his grinning eyes, you realize he knows something. Something you don't.

As so many of us, over these past months, have been wrought with fear and anger and, even, despair, as some have shed tears, day after day, fretting about what may come, this man, who has seen so much—more than seen it—who has wrestled in hand-to-hand combat with our darkest demons, stood in the lobby and smiled a smile that lit the whole room.

What does he know?

From whence does his smile come? Only a person who has faced the worst in us and fought it, and come out the other side victorious, smiles like that.

Because he knows something.

He knows how possible it is.

No matter the odds.

He knows, intimately, the awfulness we are capable of. But, more importantly, he is aware of the heights to which we sometimes ascend. His smile said, "Yes, things are tough. Once again, we face an affront to decency and humanity. But, once again, we will rise up and we will meet it. Someone will find the words."

This man's name is Clarence Jones, and he's done his part to find the words. You see, he helped Dr. King write the "I Have a Dream" speech.

It's our turn, now.

I'm reminded of a monologue from a play I was once in by George Bernard Shaw:

> The strength of a chain is no greater than its weakest link; but the greatness of a poet is the greatness of his greatest moment. Shakespeare used to get drunk. Frederick the Great ran away from a battle. But

*it was what they could rise to, not what they could sink to, that
made them great. They weren't good always; but they were good on
their day.*

It's our day. The "someone" we need is you.

If Clarence Jones is still smiling, bending still that moral arch, so must we.

———————★———————

February 5, 2017

"Repartee is something we think of twenty-four hours too late."
—MARK TWAIN

Tonight I was having a conversation when a friend tapped me on the shoulder to introduce me to someone. I turned around to see The Fonz. Henry Winkler was standing there, smiling, with his hand outstretched to shake mine. My brain tried simultaneously to say, "Oh my gosh" and "Holy cow." So, to the man who played *the* coolest character of all time I said, "Oh my cow! Nope. That's not right. You're not my cow. As you know. You know that. Ohhhh, gosh this went poorly. Nice to meet you."

———————★———————

February 7, 2017

Tonight at *Hamilton* a sweet, young girl asked her mom what a "democratic-republican" was, which is referenced in the show. In the chaos of intermission, her mother turned to me for help. I said something like, "Well, people who believe certain things tend to group together. In politics we call those groups 'parties.' Democratic-republicans were one of those groups during Hamilton's time."

The young girl said, ". . . Oh."

Then she looked at her mom and asked, "Are we democratic-republicans?"

Her mom said, "No. Um . . . well . . . I don't think so." Then she laughed and said, "I'm not sure, actually."

Which, of course, is nothing to be ashamed of. It's not easy to know "what we are." But it made me think back to the time that I first started to wonder what I was. When I was young, my family often debated politics. I heard the words "Republican" and "Democrat," and understood only that they seemed to be on opposite sides of some mysterious question my young mind couldn't quite grasp. Ronald Reagan was the president at that time, and I thought he seemed like a pretty nice guy. Warm and funny and kind. And my dad, the best man I will ever personally know, was a Republican. So, I guessed that's what I was, too.

Later, in middle school, we learned a little more about the system of governance in the United States, and the two major parties and what their "core principals" were. There were ideas in both platforms that sounded right to me. But then, later, I came across a quote by Eugene V. Debs that told me I was, in fact, a Democrat, or worse, maybe even a (cover your ears, my Republican friends) Democratic Socialist!

> *While there is a lower class, I am in it;*
> *and while there is a criminal element, I am of it;*
> *and while there is a soul in prison, I am not free.*

It refers to an innate sense of a basic connectedness between us that has always resonated with me. The feeling that we are all in this thing, whatever it is, together. And while I was fortunate enough to come into the world with an amazingly loving family, and I always had enough food and a soft, warm bed, I knew there were others on our planet and in our country and even in my immediate life that were, by simple chance, not so lucky. As Mr. Debs said, "Years ago I recognized my kinship with all living beings, and I made up my mind that I was not one bit better than the meanest on earth." There existed those who were born into poverty and heartbreak. There were some who fell asleep hungry each night. People who didn't have a mom and dad as wonderful and attentive as mine. And as comfortably as I slept in my loving home in my warm bed, by luck of the universe's draw, I couldn't help but feel that I would sleep far better if I knew everyone felt that way that night. If I could be assured that everyone was full and warm and safe and loved. Until everyone knew these things, I couldn't fully know them either.

I'm aware that this is a naive thought—that all can be cared for the way I have been. But it's a beautiful thought, too. And, as someone I know once said, "The entire universe is a beautiful thought." Thoughts are where reality starts.

So, I'm going to keep on thinking it.

That's why I'm a Democrat.

---★---

February 26, 2017

"I regard the theatre as the greatest of all art forms, the most immediate way in which a human being can share with another the sense of what it is to be a human being."

—OSCAR WILDE

During breaks in rehearsals for *Hamilton*, Lin would sit in the house and type notes on his computer. One day, I sensed he was stuck, so I sat behind him and sent very positive vibes. I'm pretty certain these vibes resulted in the song, "How Far I'll Go," from the Disney movie "Moana."

In this photo, I'm giving Lin my notes regarding the song (I thought it should be titled, "How Far I'll Go Depends Entirely On How Much Effort I Put In And How Badly I Want Whatever It Is I Think I Need, Whether or Not I Actually Do, Which I Won't Discover Until I Get It"—which he summarily rejected. So, even super-smarties don't know everything, obviously).

Here is a tip, by the way: I find (as you can see in the picture) that it's always easiest for the bartender to share their constructive critique with a person while they are holding two of their TONY Awards.

He (we) is (are) nominated for an Oscar for the song, and tonight is the ceremony. I decided to watch from home, rather than go with him. That decision was made mostly on the facts that I couldn't decide between a bow tie or classic tie, and that I wasn't invited. Good luck to you (us), Lin!

The Oscars are a noteworthy affair, if you ask me. As a tiny planet drifts on its gravitically inspired path (whatever gravity turns out to be) through an immeasurably expansive something, members of one of its subgroups of life give each other awards for who pretends the best. Really pause to think about that, if you have a minute (there's no big "Ah ha!" at the end of this story, so no rush to get there). Did you do it? If you did, and you're anything like me, or I'm anything like you (and chances are high at least one of those things will be true in some way) it might seem quite strange, all of this playacting, and how serious we are about it. But, it's also rather fantastic, and I'd argue quite a good reason to put on our finest duds and pat each other on the back a bit. To me, the Oscars are an honoring of a crazy hopeful thing, and this is it: We are a part of a species that spends enormous amounts of time and effort imagining what it feels like to be someone else. Full grown adults dress up in costumes and put on makeup and pretend *so hard* that later, other full-grown adults, who've paid to watch the made-up folks masquerade as people they aren't, in circumstances that are cultivated, forget who they really are, for a time, allowing themselves to believe so entirely the made-up people in made up situations that they weep when a fake sad thing happens to this forged person and laugh when an ultra-contrived coming together of an intricately planned "perfect moment" strikes them as on-the-spot, unsuspected, out of nowhere funny.

If an extraterrestrial intelligence were to witness this, I bet they'd be confused.

"How strange," they might say.

"How very odd to find a life form that copes with reality by duping itself."

But it is that instinct that makes us worth visiting, I should think. The desire to know what it's like to be people we aren't, and desire it *so badly* that we allow ourselves to "suspend disbelief" enough to get emotionally involved in tales we *know* are tall, is the miracle that distinguishes us from the rest of the atoms out there. What makes us unique is not the walls that separate us, but the things we use to help break them down. And that's why I love the Oscars. They aren't just an awards ceremony for great acting.

They are a celebration of sledge hammers.

———————★———————

March 12, 2017

Today at *Hamilton* I served Congressman Kevin McCarthy, the House Majority Leader, and I very possibly saved the life of someone he was with.

He asked for Peanut M&M's, which I handed to him. He looked at the package and asked, "Oh wait, these have peanuts, right?"

"They do," I said, not sure if he was kidding (he wasn't).

"They even put it in the name of the candy so that's how, ya know, that's how you know."

"One of them (whoever 'them' is) has an allergy," he said. He then asked for Reese's Pieces.

"Those are made with peanut butter," say I.

"Oh," says he.

Then we stare at each other for a moment, apparently at some type of impasse. He finally says, as though he is asking me a question, "Kit Kat?"

I tell him, "I don't think they have peanut butter, but may be made in a factory where peanuts are used. You can find out by reading the label. It's one of those pesky regulations you guys are trying to get rid of because it's too onerous for companies to comply with."

I guess your friend better hope you aren't successful in that particular deregulation, Congressman. He or she may not always have a concessionaire around to save them.

March 21, 2017

Tonight Matt Damon came to the show, and I learned that he met his wife when he walked into a Miami bar and "saw her from across the room" as she bartended. Which is pretty much exactly how it happens with me and Anna Kendrick in my imagination. Just one more thing that Matt Damon and I have in common.

---★---

March 24, 2017

"A good traveler has no fixed plans and is not intent on arriving."
—Lao Tzu

Last night at *Hamilton*, I got a surprise visit from a friend I've known since I was about ten. I still remember the first time I saw her. Having survived the first years in the new town after my parents' divorce, the summer break between fifth and sixth grade was a welcome reprieve. Negotiating the politics of elementary school had been positively exhausting, and I needed every day of the two-month vacation to recharge. But now, it was time to head back into the fray. And into a whole new fray, at that. Sixth grade meant the jump to middle school, so as the bus came into view that morning, I was particularly nervous, given the new unknown. When it pulled up, I waved to my mom, then turned and girded my loins as I went up the steps. Thankfully, a seat was empty not far from the driver, meaning I'd not have to take the long, terrible, nightmarish walk towards the back, desperately searching for a friendly face who'd allow me a spot beside them.

As we pulled away from the safety of home, I stared out of the window, looking at the passing trees and bright blue sky, and wondered if life would always feel this way. *This* tough. *This* unsure. *This* (mostly) lonely. Then, we came to a stop where a young boy and girl waited. They seemed the opposite from me, this boy and girl. They were happy and light and sure. Even at that early age they carried a confidence and carefreeness I wondered if I'd ever know. As her brother and she boarded the bus, she with her violin case and jubilant smile, I felt the stirrings of my very first crush. I'd never tell her about this, of course, but every day, as we got closer to her stop, my ever-present anxiety was replaced with anticipation. She didn't know it, but from the emotional turbulence of those first difficult years, she provided a respite.

Time passed, and through baseball and theater, I'd been able to find a voice. I was no longer the painfully timid kid I had been, and when my school chose to do Guys N' Dolls as the annual musical in my senior year, I auditioned and got cast as Nathan Detroit. And, as ever astounding fate would have it, she was chosen to play Miss Adelaide. We became good friends over the last years of high school, and especially over the course of that production. As it turned out, my ten-year-old heart had been right about her on that first day: she was beautiful in every way—most especially, the important ones. She was kind and funny and smart and good.

After the final performance of the show, we had a party at the home of one of our castmates. As she and I sat outside under the twinkling Milky Way, we looked up and wondered what life would be like when high school soon came to an end. Will things ever feel this good again? Will we ever be this happy after this night? Will the path ever again be so clear? What will we spend our lives doing? Will there be marriages and kids and jobs we love? Beneath the blanket of the night sky, we asked the questions the stars surely know by heart. I knew it in the moment, and I was right—*Someday I'll see this as one of the best nights of my life.*

Well, the years have gone by. And some of those questions have been answered. She is married to a wonderful guy, and together they have amazing children. She went on to have a wildly successful career as an actress, starring in a hit television show, and I went on to sell Skittles. And we've discovered something, too, since that night when we pondered those big questions: whether you end up on a television show or making drinks on The Great White Way, life can be challenging or sweet or, usually, both. Because happiness isn't about what you do. It's how you do it. Whatever *it* is. We didn't realize it way back when, as we stared into infinity and wondered where it would all lead, but what mattered was not the answer—it was the questioning itself. It is not the destination, but every moment of the sail that means something. The imagined goal is there only so that we might make the trip. And how lovely (though vastly different) our trips have been since that starry night. You might know Becki Newton from her fantastically funny turn as Amanda on Ugly Betty, but to me she'll always be the smiling girl carrying the violin case who gave me something to look forward to when times were tough. And who helped me realize that happiness isn't a goal; it's a way of being. And you can be it doing anything.

★

March 31, 2017

While doing an interview on CBS this morning, Lin was surprised by a video message from his eighth grade English teacher, Dr. Rembert Herbert—a surprise that brought him to tears. His teacher said, "Lin, this is your old English teacher, Dr. Herbert, here. I'm sure you didn't imagine when you were in the eighth grade and set some of 'The Chosen' to music that it would lead you where you are today." After the video played, Lin, wiping dry his eyes, said, "Dr. Herbert's the reason I'm sitting here talking to you. I wrote a musical instead of doing my homework for his class in eighth grade. He said, 'You could be good at this, and you should stop hibernating in my class, and you should be doing this.' Because we had a student-written theater club at my high school and Rembert's the one who nudged me in that direction and he sort of changed my life forever with that."

If you ask most successful people how they got where they are, how they found themselves doing what they love, chances are, beyond mentioning their parents, the story will start, "Well, there was this teacher . . ."

Last night, I learned that my middle school music teacher is going through some health issues, and many of her former students are putting together a Facebook page full of stories about her.

Given how attention averse I was back then, when the option to join the seventh-grade chorus came up, I thought, *Fantastic—with all of these people, I can easily blend in. They may not even notice I'm here.* But, on the very first day, to my horror, Mrs. Wallner was having us sing a few notes to her—individually—so she could hear what parts we were. I was sweating, absolutely drenched as it came my time to come up to the piano and sing. I did it, though, and when I was finished she said, "Yes! Good job. The way you go into the falsetto is great!" (I had no idea what "falsetto" was—and I'm pretty sure she was lying).

And that was that.

But, it wasn't.

Believe it or not, all these years later, the memory of her reaction comes often to mind. Something about the way she said, "Great" lifted my confidence and spirit in ways I can't explain.

Children are made of such very sensitive stuff. An off-handed comment of seemingly little consequence might, to them, be a lasting mental spur that gets forever stuck in their psyche.

And here's a secret: it's not just children. As we get older, we may get better at hiding it, or pretending it didn't hurt or feel good, but what we say is every bit as impactful on an adult as it is on a child. Our words can so easily be used as weapons to tear people down, or as ladders to help them reach their best selves. And we hurt or help so easily that, often, we may not even notice it.

Mrs. Wallner, I'm sure, has absolutely no recollection of this moment at the piano. Over the course of the thousands of students she has mentored, certainly this incident has been lost to the sheer volume of moments in which she's been involved. And she was just being her lovely, supporting self. But this moment, "small" and routine and easily forgotten for her, made a deep, lasting impact on me. She had no idea, but that day, with one brief sentence, she gave me a ladder.

There is someone in your life, right now, that is in a hole. They may be family, a good friend or someone you barely know—or one of your students. Give them a ladder. It's so easy, you may have already done it. Something as simple as a passing smile can be a step for someone to start climbing. If you're kind, chances are, there are an uncountable number of people out in the world, right now, better than they were before they met you—feeling, maybe, not quite as deep.

One day, many years from now, may all the ladders you've handed out come back to you and be pieced together as one, so that you may get where you'll surely be going.

You can't imagine the height of Mrs. Wallner's.

April 7, 2017

Tonight, a young man asked if I'd seen the show. I told him that, indeed, I had. "How is it?"

"It's extraordinary," I said. "Truly extraordinary."

He seemed a bit emotional—which happens all the time. People are often overcome just at having entered the theater. But for this guy, I could tell it was something different. Something more. His friend cleared it up for me when she said, "This is Taran's brother."

Taran Killam's run as King George will soon be coming to an end, and this was the first and only time his sibling, Taylor, would be able to see it. We chatted for a few minutes as I made them drinks, and by the time he left, everyone in the immediate vicinity was caught up in his ebullience and wishing him well as he bounced away to see his big brother in *Hamilton*.

At intermission, he came back. I asked him how he was enjoying the show, but his pink, watery eyes had already answered. He shook my hand and said, "I'm just . . . I'm just overwhelmed seeing him up there. I'm just totally overwhelmed with pride right now."

I know exactly how he feels. Thanks to my sisters, I, too, know that type of pride. And in a few weeks when the youngest becomes a nurse, like our mom, you won't have to ask me how the graduation ceremony went. My pink, watery eyes will have already told you.

---★---

April 13, 2017

Tonight we have Super Bowl winning quarterback Aaron Rodgers at the show. I said, "Hey Aaron. I'm Mike. It's nice to have you here. It's not often I get to hang out with someone who is on a similar level in terms of physical gifts. I'm the third baseman for the *Hamilton* softball team. You probably already know that. We exist in such rarefied air, you and I, having ability such as ours. It gets lonely at the athletic top for us, doesn't it?"

He looked at me quite seriously, and didn't speak. *Uh oh*, I thought. *He doesn't know I'm kidding. He thinks I think playing softball for Hamilton is akin to playing quarterback for the Green Bay Packers. I went and used my MFA in acting (that David Mamet warned me would never be useful) on him, and now he believes that I believe he recognizes me from playing third base in a Thursday morning summer softball league. Now he thinks he's going to have to sit here and humor me for ten minutes as we talk athletic shop. Oh well, once I clarify all this, at least I'll get to chat sports with Super Bowl winning quarterback Aaron Rodgers. This will be such a cool story to tell my kids someday!* Just then, he held up his ticket and said, "Yeah. Do you know where my seat is?"

"I don't. Sorry."

And that was my conversation with Super Bowl winning quarterback Aaron Rodgers.

────────────★────────────

May 24, 2017

Tonight at *Hamilton*, we had one of the "real housewives" come to the bar. It occurred to me, as I watched her interactions with those around her, that the definition of "real" has changed since I was a kid. I remember reading this from the Velveteen Rabbit:

> *"Real isn't how you are made," said the Skin Horse.*
> *"It's a thing that happens to you.*
> *When a child loves you for a long, long time, not just to play with,*
> *but REALLY loves you, then you become Real."*
> *"Does it hurt?" asked the Rabbit.*
> *"Sometimes," said the Skin Horse, for he was always truthful.*
> *"When you are Real you don't mind being hurt."*
> *"Does it happen all at once, like being wound up,"*
> *he asked, "or bit by bit?"*
> *"It doesn't happen all at once," said the Skin Horse. "You become. It*
> *takes a long time. That's why it doesn't happen often to people who*
> *break easily, or have sharp edges, or who have to be carefully kept.*
> *Generally, by the time you are Real, most of your hair has been*
> *loved off, and your eyes drop out and you get loose in the joints and*
> *very shabby. But these things don't matter at all, because once you*
> *are Real you can't be ugly, except to people who don't understand."*

Recalling that, it was clear there was little real about this "real housewife" who glistened and gleamed in splendid make-up and glittering clothes, or the brief, superficial interactions she was having. "Real" happens, often when no one is looking, and is rarely captured on film.

Phones were lifted for selfie after selfie, and those entering the theater wondered what all the fuss was about, while cameras continued to flicker and flash. As the lights lit her up more and more, people who didn't even know who she was began to want photos as well, assuming it must be important in some way, and rushed to be next in line. Meanwhile, a girl came in with her family, and cried.

She didn't even notice the hoopla on the other end of the lobby, as she immediately looked up toward the monitor on the wall showing the stage. The tears were the joyful kind, I found out, when her little brother reached up to pat her on the shoulder and she smiled and picked him up (as far as her three-and-a-half-foot frame would allow) and said, "I'm okay. I just can't believe this is real." She'd buried her face in his jacket, leaving her tears, and a good amount of mucus (which grossed me out some) behind. But their parents, who hadn't noticed the kerfuffle going on up ahead, staring only at their kids, seemed to enjoy it, as the dad happily wiped the boogers away.

I wish everyone there could have seen her tear and snot-strewn face. That would have been a picture worth having.

Don't be too fooled by the shiny stuff.

What is most truly real will most likely not shine at all (and maybe even be a little bit gross). Except to those that understand.

———————★———————

May 26, 2017

When I was about four years old, my parents discovered that I had an inexplicable love for the song "I Can't Smile Without You," by Barry Manilow. Any time it came on the radio, I'd ask my mom to "Put it up!"

"Please," she'd remind me.

"Please."

"Raise the volume," my dad would correct.

"Okay, okay, PLEASE, RAISE the VOLUME."

Then we'd listen to the rest of the song. And if we'd arrived at our destination, but the song wasn't over, we'd stay in the car until it was. It was almost like I'd had some past life connection to it. What four-year-old's favorite artist was Barry Manilow?

Regardless of the reason for my love of his music, my dad, when I was about five, found out that Barry was performing in Pennsylvania.

The greatest thrill of my then young life was to take drives with my dad. We usually had no destination. We took the trips not to get somewhere, but to be somewhere. This one day he said we'd be taking a longer drive than usual. One we'd need a map for—and I got to be the navigator. This, of course, was long before the internet, and earlier still than consumer GPS systems (I'd find out later that my dad, being a FedEx driver, had an encyclopedic knowledge of the roadway system throughout the Northeast. We didn't need that map at all. But he let me think we did, and it was awesome). As though the long drive we took, just the two of us, wasn't spectacular enough, he told me on the way that we were headed to see Barry Manilow in concert!

It was an outdoor venue, and we were way at the back of the lawn, so far that Barry couldn't be discerned from the piano. But it didn't matter. It was the best day I'd ever had up to that point.

Getting to hear "I Can't Smile Without You," live, sitting in my dad's lap on a blanket on the great lawn, was, well . . . perfect.

As the years passed, I grew to love Manilow even more. Throughout my adolescence, music brought me comfort. As I've mentioned, the early years weren't always easy for me. Being so unusually shy made me an easy target for the other, more popular kids to aim their popular behavior. I tried to not let my classmates ever see how they affected me, but they did. It was such a strange thing, to walk out of my home and go to school. At home I was hugged and loved and made to feel as though I was an essential part of the universe. But at school it was the opposite. At school I was told I was weird and wrong and not worthy of . . . whatever it is people got when they are accepted. Luckily, there was one other student who was similarly treated, and he and I formed a bond—the kind, I imagined, my grandfather forged in the trenches he told me about. So, it was just me and my pal Eddie (who is now a professor of child psychology, go figure) roughing the childhood storm together. And Barry! Barry was there for me, too, and if I ever had a particularly bad, bully-filled day, I don't mind admitting (now), I'd come home and listen to "I Made it Through the Rain":

> *When friends are hard to find*
> *And life seems so unkind*
> *Sometimes you feel afraid.*
> *Just aim beyond the clouds*
> *And rise above the crowds*
> *And start your own parade.*

I'd listen to those words, and take them to heart. It seemed that Barry had been through, I'd thought, *exactly* what I had been struggling with, and he turned out pretty darned good! *Someday,* I thought, *I will start my own parade.* Just like Barry. *Someday,* that song made me feel, *I'll be strong enough to do that.*

I remained a Barry Manilow fan all through high school. "Mandy" helped get me through my first heartbreak. To this day, if a Manilow song comes on my radio, I turn it all the way up and sing it at the top of my lungs. My oldest and closest friends joke with me about my "Barry thing" still.

Tonight, at *Hamilton*, I met "The Man Who Writes the Songs."

And it was surprisingly emotional for me. Here's why: I realized, meeting him, in a single moment, that though his music is full of joy and love and awesomeness, and it most certainly made me feel less hopeless on so many of those tough days, it was you, Dad, who "Got me through the rain."

How I wish I could tell you that in person.

Seeing Barry live back then was amazing. But it didn't compare to the drive there.

June 27, 2017

Lin is in town at the moment, and he stopped by the bar before the show to say, "Hi" (and to get a soda. But mostly, for sure, to say, "Hi.") He's a truly nice person. You might think with everything that's happened to him over the past few years, some of the constant adulation would have gone to his head. But it hasn't. He is the same guy today as the one I met all those years ago when we were getting ready to bring *In The Heights* into the Rodgers. But, he is a pretty big deal now, especially on Broadway, and it's no longer simple for him to just walk down the street. Therefore, he does what he can to disguise himself when out and about, and most definitely when at the theater, not wanting to cause a scene. So, during the now more rare occasions that he visits, the audience doesn't know they are watching the show alongside Lin.

But tonight, there was a boy.

He's probably about ten, I'd guess. He came up to the bar with his parents, and it was immediately clear that being here was far more meaningful than it might be for a typical kid of his age. It was also clear that life may not always be easy for this young man. He's the type of child that wears his heart on his sleeve. The sensitive sort. Knowing how tough, sometimes, children can be to each other, my heart broke a little when he said to me, "I just can't believe I'm really here. This is the best night of my life. I've listened to the album nine-and-a-half times today."

It was something about the "and-a-half" time he listened that really got me in the cockles.

His parents smiled, but they sensed the crowd building behind them and worried they were taking too much time. "It's fine," I mouthed.

Then, I let this boy in on the secret.

I signaled for him to come closer, and in a whisper said, "Listen, this is just between you and me, okay? Don't tell anyone else."

And his breath quickened as he said, "Yes, definitely," thrilled at the prospect of what I was going to say.

"Lin is here tonight. Be on the look-out for him."

His eyes flew open wide, and almost let some tears come, it seemed.

"No way. No way. Is this real?"

"Yup," I said. "No one knows but you."

And the joy he was already feeling now reached ecstatic levels.

As he bounced away, peepers peeled, I knew there'd be days that aren't easy for him. But I knew, also, that he'd be okay. Anyone with the capacity to feel that type of joy is going to make it.

And help the world make it, too.

Sorry to blow your cover, Lin. I promise, though, it was worth it.

————————— ★ —————————

July 14, 2017

"He made us laugh. Hard. Every time you saw him. On television, movies, night clubs, arenas, hospitals, homeless shelters, for our troops overseas, and even in a dying girl's living room for her last wish. He made us laugh. Big time. I spent many happy hours with Robin on stage. I mean, the brilliance was astounding, the relentless energy was kind of thrilling . . . I used to think that if I could put a saddle on him and stay on for eight seconds I was going to do okay [. . .] It's very hard to talk about him in the past, because he was so present in all of our lives. For almost forty years, he was the brightest star in the comedy galaxy. But while some of the brightest of our celestial bodies are actually extinct now, their energy long since cooled, miraculously, because they float in the heavens, so far away from us now, their beautiful light will continue to shine on us, forever. And the glow will be so bright, it'll warm your heart, it'll make your eyes glisten, and you'll think to yourselves, 'Robin Williams. What a concept.'"

—Billy Crystal

On the train today, a lovely woman noticed the *Hamilton* softball uniform I was wearing (that I'd squeezed into—this diet is still not taking full effect, for some reason—is it all the ice cream? Who can say?), and she asked how I was involved with the show. After telling her, we had a great conversation about the candescent experience that is *Hamilton*, and live theater, in general. Eventually, she said that what she loves to see most is a comedy. Laughing together with strangers, she thinks, is particularly important for a healthy world, and comedies shouldn't be given "such short shrift" by the critics. The conversation turned to Robin Williams, who left us three years ago in August. I told her about the surreal experience of first getting to meet Robin when he performed his stand-up special, "Weapons of Mass Destruction" at The Town Hall theater in New York.

Through some lovely twist of fate, I had gotten the job of setting up his dressing room. All day long I'd been running from store to store, picking up last minute items—like the towels he'd want when he got off stage to wipe off the prodigious amount of sweat his otherworldly vitality would create during the hour-and-a-half of manic comic mastery. I put the final touches on his dressing room, then headed downstairs to take the seat the production had so kindly saved for me. However, being a bit late getting to the stage level, I couldn't go into the house, as cameras were rolling, and the show was about to begin. So, in one of the most fortuitous late arrivals of my life, I stood by Robin in the right wing, as he awaited his cue to enter. It was just me, Robin, and a stage hand. Robin noticed something about the stage hand's shoes that struck him as amusing, and it set him off on a divinely inspired comedic tangent. It was stunning and almost overwhelming to be a part of. I was simultaneously enjoying the show, and outside of my body watching me enjoy the show. To be two feet from this whirlwind of mesmerizing virtuosity was nearly too much for my consciousness to wrap itself around. As I said, he was moments away from being given the nod for his entrance, when every other performer I've ever known would be getting focused and prepared in some way. Especially if the show they were about to perform was to be recorded for posterity and broadcast to the world on HBO. But Mr. Williams, instead, spent those moments before his entrance to provide some laughs to two guys he didn't know. He gave the same superhuman energy to two guys standing in the dark of the wings, without a single camera on him, that he was about to give the world.

You've probably heard stories like this about Robin. About him brightening strangers lives at a time they so needed it, such as in an out of the way diner late one night, where a family had gathered after a day spent burying a loved one, or, as Billy Crystal would remind us, in a dying girl's living room for her last wish. It didn't matter if you were two guys standing beside him right before he was to take the stage, or a world-wide audience; Robin Williams wanted to make you feel better. Any chance he got.

A few years after I had this experience with him, Robin made his Broadway debut at the Rodgers where he befriended Fran. Here's the thing, though: Robin meant a great deal to me well before I'd get to spend these magical moments with him in person. For reasons that run deep, when I learned of his passing, I was devastated. Here's what I wrote within minutes of getting the news, before we knew of his crushing diagnosis:

I was moved to tears when I heard about Robin Williams' passing, and this is why: he changed the universe for me when I was five. At five, I had a great deal of difficulty (still do) watching the news. I couldn't (can't) bear the reality I saw on television. The reality was this: I hold membership with a subset of life that sometimes does intentionally horrible things to each other. *Why, why, why?* was always my thought. *Why God? I want so badly to believe this all means something, that you, whatever you are, are there. And, more importantly, you are good. But if you made us, and we are like this, have this terrible stuff inside of us, then doesn't that mean . . . well, what does that mean? And if not, if it, the bad stuff, somehow came from somewhere else, why let it happen? WHY?* And I didn't need to go as far as the news to see this awful reality. It was right there in my own little world. I would see children being cruel to each other on the playground. I mean, really trying to hurt each other—not physically (though sometimes in that way, too) but in far worse ways. They were trying to hurt each other's being. Trying to make each other feel bad. This type of thing absolutely rocked me to my core. Then, I met Mork.

Mork was from another planet. An alien. But, somehow, he had the humanness I was looking for. Something about what Robin Williams did through that character felt more real to me than the stuff on the news. I instantly recognized humor, his humor in particular, as being from a "higher" place. In my young mind, this type of humor (that is never at anyone's expense) was from the God I wanted so badly to believe in and feel. This thing that Robin Williams did softened people. It connected us. It was made of love, whatever that means. I felt it as truth. And it was so much more clear and powerful than the news. For me, in fact, it blew the news away. It turned the news into a paper tiger. That stuff wasn't real. Mork was. Robin Williams' desire to make me laugh was. I was so relieved to discover that the universe had this in it. It comes in all different forms and appearances, but Robin was the first for me. Then I found Richard Pryor and Lucille Ball and Dudley Moore and Faulty Towers. But it started with Robin Williams. And I'm delighted to say that when, years later, I met him in person, he lived up in every way to my childhood picture of him. He was sweet and lovely and unbelievably fast and funny and generous with his spirit. In his eyes, I did indeed see and feel Mork, the alien who showed me the humanity I'd been seeking.

When asked by James Lipton, "If heaven exists, what would you like to hear God say when you arrive at the Pearly Gates?" Robin Williams said:

"'There is seating near the front. The concert begins at 5, it'll be Mozart, Elvis and one of your choosing.' Or to know that there's laughter. That would be a great thing. Just to hear God say, 'Two Jews walk into a bar . . . '"

Well, Robin (and I'll call you Robin now that you know how close we are), if there wasn't laughter before, there certainly is now. But oh, how I'll miss it here. So desperately. Because those fears I had as a child begin to creep back in, from time to time. The fear that the world is not a good place. The gnawing suspicion that we are doomed because our humanity has been found lacking. I'll miss having you there to stand in front of the madness and evaporate it instantly with a joke. I'll miss those moments when God whispered to me, through you, through your joy of connecting people with guffaws, "It's all okay." I'll miss you shining your light into the evil, revealing nothing but a shadow.

How I wish I had told you, face to face, what you meant to me. A total stranger. We'd not met, yet you sculpted how the world looked to me. You made it a softer place. A more loving and joyful place. You gave me hope that it did, indeed, mean something. Even the bad bits. It was all part of a plan I was far too small to comprehend. But because of you, I had no doubt it existed. You gave me peace. I'm sorry we couldn't give the same to you. If only Robin Williams had a Robin Williams.

So, here is my deepest wish: that when you get to the Pearly Gates, every laugh you ever stirred, every joy you ever bestowed, every fear you eased and comfort you brought, hits you with a mighty force. I hope your newly enlarged spirit will be granted the ability to feel what it is you did here. I want you to be given, in a moment, the totality of what you gave. No human could handle this type of overwhelming love all at once, of course. But Mork could. And now, I pray, you can. And I hope you get there right in the middle of God on stage telling his joke. But, as it turns out, it's your joke. "So, then Robin says, two Jews walk into a bar . . ." Then He'll notice you, and trail off. "Robin, you're early! Come up here. Tell them that thing you said. I don't do it right. Folks, let's welcome Robin back. Robin Williams, everybody." And the stage that's been set up is for you. And there is Mozart in the front row, elbowing Elvis in the side with every laugh.

Thank you, Robin. Thank you thank you thank you. You were one of my angels, sent from God to let me know I was right; love is the animating force, and laughter is what it sounds like.

That's the real stuff. No darkness or fear stands up to that.

Godspeed.

> *Edit: it was later learned that Robin had been fighting a terrible, unimaginable battle with a particularly devastating form of the already devastating disease known as Parkinson's. What he so valiantly tried to live with is known as Lewy Body Dementia, and is characterized by over forty symptoms, any of which, by itself, would be distressing in the utmost, and Robin had almost all of them. As his wife later said, "Robin was exhausted from the terror coming from his brain. He took it before it could take any more of him."*

July 30, 2017

Tonight at *Hamilton*, I met Theresa Caputo, who is best known these days as the "Long Island Medium." My friends will know that this is of interest to me, since I'm involved in a documentary project exploring "mediumship," and whether or not it's a genuine phenomenon that science can't yet explain. Theresa has done many things in her life that are not thought to be possible within our current scientific paradigm. Stuff that, when carefully looked at, will blow any skeptical, but open mind, a bit further asunder. The things some of the people who claim to be "mediums" do is astounding. And certainly, in Theresa's case, it can garner lots of attention. But what I'd like to point out about my evening is not meeting Theresa Caputo, one of the people currently best-known for practicing the phenomenon I'm studying. What I'd like to highlight is the interaction I had with her husband, Larry.

Theresa and Larry were allowed into the theater before the general public (which we often do for security reasons with people who are public figures). While Theresa looked at merchandise, I made a drink for her husband. When he attempted to hand me money to pay for it, I said, "That's on me." And Larry looked at me and said:

"No, come on, really?"

"Yes," I said. "You've helped bring comfort to lots of people. It's on me."

Hearing that, he looked, almost, like he was going to cry. Instead of giving any kind of verbal thanks, he simply shook my hand.

Later, when the show had ended and Larry and Theresa were leaving, Larry made a point to come over to me once more, and, as he flashed the peace sign, quietly said, "Thank you."

Hamilton is a phenomenon. It's an incomparable creative feat that has become a part of the zeitgeist. And the stuff Theresa does is utterly amazing. She appears to deliver messages from the next world back to this one. But years from now, when I reflect on this night, the evening I met a woman displaying an ability beyond anything science currently accepts as possible, at a show that changed the world, what I'll most remember is a soft-spoken man being moved at hearing that he'd brought comfort to someone. Whether or not what Theresa does is real, and no matter how large *Hamilton* will one day loom in the annals of musical theater history, what I'll hold in my heart about tonight is the look I saw in one man's eyes after I'd told him he'd helped make a difference to me. That's what matters, friends. And you don't have to be a lyrical sage or communicator with the "other side" to do it. You make a difference every time you're kind. Every. Single. Time.

---★---

September 7, 2017

Tonight at *Hamilton,* I met Steve Kerr, coach of the Golden State Warriors basketball team. I said, "Coach, I played a little b-ball in my day. I can probably help you guys out. I know I look short. And chubby. And slow. And forty. But I'm a great shot."

I then went to pour his wife a glass of wine.

And missed the cup.

In my defense, I was doing a "no look" pour, which always impresses. Except when you miss. From an inch away. In front of the coach of the NBA's most recent championship team.

October 1, 2017

"Hello, babies. Welcome to Earth. It's hot in the summer and cold in the winter. It's round and wet and crowded. At the outside, babies, you've got about a hundred years here. There's only one rule that I know of, babies—God damn it, you've got to be kind."
—KURT VONNEGUT,
GOD BLESS YOU, MR. ROSEWATER

Tonight at *Hamilton*, a man walked up to the bar and asked my bar partner and pal, Marie, for a drink. After making it she asked, "Would you like some lime in that?" To which he replied (with tears welling in his eyes as he glanced up from a text message received on his phone) "I'm sorry, I'm going through a terrible divorce."

At first, I must admit, we found ourselves containing an uncomfortable smile. The sheer incongruity between the question—"Would you like some lime?"—and the tearful response—"I'm going through a terrible divorce," was enough to throw us.

There, at *Hamilton*, where most in attendance were having the time of their lives, this man stood in the lobby as his life fell apart.

It ain't easy bein' a person.

We're born into this existence, and given just enough brains to understand that we can't understand.

We do what we can to make peace with that remarkably unsettling set up, and pull together bits of the mystery that make us feel good, using them to build a nest against the cold uncertainty, and cozy up our corner of things.

With perseverance and some luck, many of us find others to share the questions with. And often, we eventually stumble upon one "special someone." The bond with that someone can be so powerful that it becomes the nest. The one place where love is sure, and things make sense—which is so desperately needed, since things don't make sense.

And then, sometimes, even the nest comes undone. The one thing we knew, the only certainty in the great, vast uncertainty, is revealed to be made of straw.

Sometimes, at the moment that happens to someone, you, by chance, are there. Asking about limes.

Be kind, pals.

We're all in a nearly impossible situation. The fact that we carry on as well as we do given the context, is nothing short of flabbergasting.

We all lose our nest, at some point, in some way. If a person happens to be losing theirs, you may not know it. It may not be outwardly obvious. A lot of that stuff takes place on the inside.

Sometimes, though, it happens at *Hamilton,* in the midst of people having the time of their lives—their nests, for the moment, intact. And you reach out from the abyss to share your shattered heart with the person who is most near, who is questioning you about fruit.

It ain't easy bein' a person.

So, be kind. You might be the branch someone grasps as they fall.

---- ★ ----

October 3, 2017

*"Thus I, gone forth as spiders do
In spider's web a truth discerning,
Attach one silken strand to you
For my returning."*

—E.B. WHITE

Jimmy Kimmel, the host of a late-night comedy show, has, of all people, become a voice of reason as we live through the surreal experience of having a reality star as our president.

Last night, Jimmy gave an emotional response to the tragedy of the mass shooting in Las Vegas—which happens to be his hometown. As you'd expect, there are plenty of people out there asking why a comedian is sticking his nose into political affairs. I won't get too far into the idea that the Court Jester has long been the one who speaks truth to power. Just ask King Lear. But I will tell you what little I know of Jimmy Kimmel personally.

Marie and I have a friend, Daniella, who lost her mom a couple of years ago. Her mom absolutely loved Jimmy. Daniella lives in Orlando, but as fate would have it, she happened to be in New York visiting Marie exactly one year to the day of her mom's passing.

While Marie and I were at work at *Hamilton* that night, Daniella found things to do to stay occupied in the city.

And, wouldn't you know it, exactly a year to the day after losing her mom, the universe happened to put her mom's absolute favorite celebrity in the house.

Marie and I generally leave before the show is quite over. On this night, though, the universe caused us to have some issues with our inventory software program. Which made us late.

When finally we were finished, well after the show had ended, Marie rounded a corner in the empty and darkened lobby and nearly ran into Jimmy Kimmel, who it turned out, the universe had kept behind to meet with the cast.

Upon bumping into him, a flustered, huge-hearted Marie quickly told Jimmy the story about her friend who happened to be in town who had lost her mom exactly one year ago to the day and to whom Jimmy was one of the best things on Earth.

To which Jimmy asked, "Well, where is your friend now?"

Marie explained that she was somewhere in midtown. Then Jimmy said, "Can you call her and have her come? I'll wait."

Which he did. And she came. And it was . . . exactly what you think it was.

That's what I know of Jimmy Kimmel. A guy who saw a young girl that thought of his presence that night as a sign from her mom—and who wasn't going to let her mom down.

When you see Jimmy cry—which happens a lot lately—know it's not an act. Those are genuine tears from a big, breaking heart.

———————— ★ ————————

October 13, 2017

Before we opened the house at *Hamilton* last night, the bathroom door at the back of the lobby swung out as I approached it. A person emerged, and I let out an audible gasp. Standing in front of me was Shaquille O'Neil. I stared in astonishment, truly dumbfounded by the sheer physical mass of the former NBA superstar. I tried to say something witty and intelligent, and what came out was, "I mean . . . gosh." Not feeling as though that was enough, thinking I needed to be a bit more clear, I attempted to say something else, but instead repeated it: "Gosh."

At which Shaq winked an eyelid the size of my head.

What a fantastically diverse universe. It's got trees and hippos and ants and giraffes and platypuses and three-toed sloths and flying squirrels and flightless penguins and the odds-defying, "shouldn't"-be-possible, light-producing life in the depths of the ocean that we can barely comprehend, and who knows what else we've yet to find (or will find us) out there.

How is it that nature, using just a few shades, just protons and neutrons and electrons as her paint, made all of this?

How could the very same species of life, instructed by just protons and neutrons and electrons, gathered by some force into double helix strands of DNA, which use other protons and neutrons and electrons, and nothing discernible else, molded by that force into molecules of protein to carry out those instructions, contain tiny little me, and great big Shaq?

When you really think about it, I mean, well, just . . . gosh.

What a wonderful world.

---★---

November 4, 2017

Tonight at *Hamilton*, we had The Queen of Soul.

When Aretha Franklin performed "A Natural Woman" at the 2015 Kennedy Center Honors, President Obama could be seen wiping away tears. He said later, "Nobody embodies more fully the connection between the African-American spiritual, the blues, R&B, rock and roll—the way that hardship and sorrow were transformed into something full of beauty and vitality and hope." (If you haven't seen that performance, watch it right now!)

In a country divided, much more so, even, than it is now—a country where people with a certain shade of skin had to read in a designated place in the library and sit at the back of the bus and in the upper level of theaters and attend "separate but equal" schools and use only certain pools and phone booths and not walk through public parks and endure indignities of unimaginable varieties—in the midst of all of that, Aretha Franklin opened her mouth and made that sound.

Every now and again, something happens to challenge our conceptions of reality. Sometimes, we run up against something, or something runs into us with such a force that it puts a crack in the boundary of what we think we know, and peering through the breach, our understanding of what is gets expanded. When Aretha sang, she stopped us in our tracks, wresting attention immediately from whatever earthly endeavor we'd been engaged in. Her voice seemed to emanate from somewhere beyond that wall, and every time she used it, a piece of the border chipped away.

Aretha Franklin gave us the sound of her soul, and with it she changed the world.

She was the first woman to be inducted into the Rock and Roll Hall of Fame.

Her voice was declared a natural resource by the state of Michigan.

She's even got an asteroid named after her.

She's been given the Grammy Lifetime Achievement Award, the National Medal of Arts and the Presidential Medal of Freedom.

And, after tonight, she's been given a free pack of Peppermint Life Savers by me. (Where do you suppose she places that on her list of accomplishments?)

How amazing, to be in the presence of such history. Such power and grace. And such hope. Because of people like Aretha, we've made it through darker times than the one we're in. And we'll make it through this one, too.

———————— ★ ————————

November 24, 2017

"Every child comes with the message that God is not yet discouraged of man."

—Rabindranath Tagore

I'm thankful for the kid on the train.

Last night, an old man in a wheelchair rolled in at the 125th street stop in Harlem. A young boy (who would later tell this man that he was four) asked immediately and loudly, to his mother's minor embarrassment,

> "Why are you in that chair?"
> To which the man responded, "Because I have no legs."
> "You have no legs?!?" shouted the boy. "Why?"
> "Because I was in an accident and they had to take them away
>   in an operation."
> "Oh," said the boy. "It's okay, I'll push you where you need to go!"
> The man said, "You will?"
> "Yeah, we'll have fun!"

The boy's mother's minor embarrassment turned immediately into pride (as well as some teary eyes—and she wasn't alone). The boy and the old, legless man became fast friends, and talked until we reached the boy's stop. As he left, he smiled at the man—"Don't worry, someone will always be around to push you," he said waving goodbye.

After the door closed, the man said to the people standing and sitting around him (it was a packed train) "That's a good one, that boy."

Life is going to happen to that boy.

He'll get pulled this way and that, and he'll stumble and tumble and fall down and get hurt. Life may make him bitter and mean and sad. He may sometimes hurt people. Even those he loves. But, I hope he'll always remember that when he started, he wanted to help a stranger who had no legs get where he needed to go. He was "a good one."

That's how we start.
That's who we are. Before too much life happens to us.
But I believe we're always in there, somewhere.
Take heart;
You're a good one, too :)
Happy Thanksgiving.

December 21, 2017

I just served Sean Spicer.

As I snapped the lid onto his souvenir cup he said, "Oh, a top. I like that."

I said, "I don't give one to everybody—just people I think are going to make a historic mess."

He didn't find it very amusing.

He did, though, leave a $5 tip. Which he said is the biggest tip anyone, anywhere, at any time has ever been given.

---★---

December 30, 2017

"Everybody is worth everything."
—MAYA ANGELOU

Tonight at *Hamilton*, we had a ridiculously wealthy guest. He made his billions in the pharmaceutical industry. Billions. With a "B." This guy was really nice. I mean that—he seemed, in the short time that we were together, like a good person. He was kind and generous with his energy. And with his wallet. He tipped our security guard $1,000 like it was nothing, and one of our bartenders $500. Which was great. The security guard and the bartenders went back to their homes with hundreds of dollars more than they would have.

On the way to those houses, about one-hundred feet from the Richard Rodgers Theater, the security guard and the bartenders and I passed an old man sleeping on the street. I think he was old, that is. I can't be certain, because I never saw his face. I'm only guessing he was old from the tuft of grey hair that had escaped from beneath the donated, dirty blankets the man had bound himself in as he huddled over a sidewalk grate from which steam occasionally erupted—an unknown process below the street providing the only intermittent warmth available. While he shivered there on the sidewalk, I quietly slipped a dollar, not enough to buy a coffee, into his broken cup. A block further, the scene repeated with a different old man on a different grate. Between the theater and Grand Central, I passed seven people sleeping on the street. It's twelve degrees tonight in New York City.

It was so nice of that billionaire to tip us all so well. Truly—it was. I have no doubt his heart felt good handing out that money.

Billionaire.

A *billionaire.*

The brain makes poor sense of large numbers. At a certain point, it lumps it all into one category: a lot. But thinking about the CEO and what the zeros in his bank account actually mean, I came upon a way of conceptualizing it that put it a bit more into perspective for me; a million seconds is about 12 days. A billion seconds is 31 *years.* That's how much wildly more a billion is than a million.

157

But the only conceptualization that matters is the human one. What it means, in human terms, is this: the man I met tonight has far more money than he could spend. Ever. It's more than he will be able to use, no matter how many security guards and bartenders he tips. He could give nearly every person he sees $1,000 for the rest of his life, and it would make no difference to the amount of money he has, as perceived by his and our brains. He will simply not be able to consume that much for himself.

We have set up a system where some people can have many thousands of times more than they could possibly use in hundreds of lifetimes, while others have so little they need to sleep outside, in temperatures of twelve degrees, huddled on grates, shivering, struggling to just keep breathing, praying for the relief from the cold that only sleep might bring—in this lifetime. Right now. Right now, billions of dollars sit in a nice man's bank account, accumulating with an ever-increasing rapidity, while the seven people I passed, and so many more, shiver on a street.

The man I saw, old and cold and quaking, isn't sleeping on a sidewalk grate because there isn't enough room for him in a warm place. He wasn't cold because there isn't heat.

He was cold because we didn't give it to him.

This can't be the best way.

It just can't.

January 30, 2018

Today a young girl entered the train and took a seat close to where I was sitting. I travel in the "Quiet Car," something Metro North has initiated for passengers looking to read or get work done or just sit in silence for a bit.

This young girl didn't seem to notice the "Quiet Car" signs, or if she did (which seemed more likely) she simply ignored them. She chewed her gum loudly and blew bubbles and had an ongoing phone conversation, with volume enough for all in the vicinity to hear. Other passengers traded "these kids today have no respect" looks, and I found myself closer to "old-man-on-the-porch-get-off-my-lawn" than "let kids be kids."

Meanwhile, across from me, a woman without sight found her seat with some difficulty. Older, mature adults like me, the ones respecting the "Quiet Car" signs, watched as a few people, unaware of her lack of sight, blew past her. There was some frustration evident on the woman's face as she used her probing cane to locate where to sit. I nearly asked her if I could offer assistance, but then didn't, worried it might make it seem like I didn't think she could do it herself, as I'm certain she does every day. So, I said nothing.

The young girl continued to blow bubbles and talk loudly and generally annoy the older, respectful, more mature passengers.

A few stops later, the woman came to hers, which also happened to be the young lady's destination.

I watched as, again, the woman struggled a bit to find the door. And, again, I wondered if I should help. But didn't. Neither did almost anyone else.

Almost.

Through the window I saw the woman stop on the platform, allowing the crowd to pass. We were in Stamford, CT, which is a big station with lots of stairways and tracks and different levels, and I couldn't imagine how she'd discern where to go.

I should have helped her, I thought. I felt immediate guilt as the doors closed and I saw her struggling to probe her way.

And then, the young, bubble-blowing, disrespectful kid who'd been on our lawns, walked up to the woman and gently took her arm. I couldn't hear what was said, but the enormous smile on the woman's face was clear.

As the train pulled away, I watched the two chat, as the young woman guided, with great love and deep respect, the older woman towards her destination.

"These kids have no respect"—for the quiet car. But greater respect for what actually matters than anyone else on it today.

I wish I knew who that girl's parents are. I'd like to tell them my first impression of their daughter.

And what she taught me about first impressions.

And how there are much more important things than quiet.

March 29, 2018

Tonight at *Hamilton*, we had Jonathan Van Ness from the reboot of *Queer Eye*, a new series on Netflix in which five men who identify as gay or queer spend a week with a person nominated by someone close to them who they believe needs general life coaching sort of help from the "Fab Five." The episodes are often quite emotional, as the attention and care the guys give seem to help people genuinely blossom, and for that reason my friend and bar partner, Andy, and I are big fans of the show (and of the original).

I don't get star struck these days, having lived and worked so long in New York City, but I have to say when Andy gave me the signal tonight, I felt that old flutter. The "signal" is the code word Andy, Marie and I early on decided we'd use to alert each other when we see someone in the crowd we feel the others would be interested to know is there, and we don't want to be too obvious about it. We went with "rochambeau," the code Hamilton used during a battle at Yorktown, and that is referenced in the show. The system isn't perfect, as often we're so busy the code isn't heard, leaving customers wondering why we are repeating the same strange word, louder and louder, and then finally throwing a piece of ice at our bar partner's head. When the ice hit me this evening, and I looked over to find Andy serving Jonathan, I felt glee. See, one of the multitude of perfect things Andy is, is gay, and knowing how he feels about *Queer Eye*, and Jonathan in particular, it was thrilling to watch them speaking.

I'd turned just in time to see Andy say something to Jonathan I couldn't quite hear, but which caused a reaction impossible to miss in a woman standing to the side. Later, I would learn this woman is Jonathan's mom, who he'd brought as his date. Whatever Andy said elicited from her the sort of expression one makes when your emotions surprise you, and control of the facial muscles is lost. As soon as we had a lull, I told Andy about her effusive response, and asked what he'd said to cause such a reaction. He was so caught up in excitement that he couldn't recall his exact words, but the gist had been his expressing to Jonathan what he meant to him, and thanking him for making the world a better place.

Who knows what this woman watched her son go through, and how deeply she worried as he navigated the sometimes cold and hurtful waters a young gay person often faces.

But tonight, it was all worth it. She got to hear, firsthand, how profoundly her son had affected someone—her ridiculously strong son, who said to the wide world "This is me. And I am exactly right." And the world had no choice but to listen.

I've cried during each episode of the new *Queer Eye* series, but the image of Jonathan's mom placing her hand over her heart while directly learning of her son's impact may take the cake.

Edit: When we met Jonathan, it was before the show had taken off. Today, he's a household name, helping people all over the world be who they are. So, just imagine his mom's face now.

———————————★———————————

April 23, 2018

Given the way the survivors of the Parkland school shooting have handled themselves, and the astounding movement they've single-handedly generated, it's easy to forget how young they are. Upon their shoulders this great task has been placed. Their names have become household, and not always are they spoken with admiration. These survivors have had to contend with enormous powers that stand in direct opposition to what they are fighting for, and have been faced with the sort of unfiltered hatred borne in the instinctual and uncontemplated lizard portion of our brains, the likes of which doesn't often slink out into the light—no amount of experience or maturity can prepare a person, let alone a kid, for receiving threats for expressing a desire for common sense change. And yet, so prepared they seem.

Last night, though, I got a peek behind the public facade. As David Hogg, one of the more visible faces of the Never Again movement, walked through the lobby of *Hamilton* during intermission with his mom, her instinct for protectiveness was evident. It was apparent that what this young man has received has not always been support. So, when it became clear that I recognized him, his mom immediately placed her arm around her son, waiting to see, I think, where I stood.

I reached out my hand to shake his and said, "You, young man, are changing the world." And his mom let go of his shoulder and her shield went down and her eyes became wet.

"Thank you," she said. "Thank you."

The *Hamilton* cast signed posters and wrote letters to the Parkland students, many of whom are involved in their high school's theater program. The kids look up to these Broadway actors; if only they knew how these actors stand in awe of them. It is a beautiful thing to watch; these children, the ones who have faced down the barrel of a bullet-spraying gun, these kids who should be the most afraid among us, are answering instead, with love. While our elected officials cower to the NRA, as these congressional cowards bandy about the idea of adding *more* guns to the equation, the people who should be the most afraid, these kids, are standing up and speaking out—and doing it with grace. One of the students, when a commentator tried to put the blame on the security guard (who surely was afraid and confused and unsure what to do and, just, human when the firestorm broke out) stopped the commentator and said, "There was nothing that man could have done. If he'd come in and started firing, he would just have hit more kids. Don't point the finger at him." This child cut right through the commentator's faulty premise. It was powerful to watch truth from the "mouth of a babe" stop the questioner in her tracks. How can such maturity have been fostered in so few years? This question was forefront in my mind tonight after talking with young David and his mom. After a brief chat, I offered them anything they wanted, on the house. And David's eyes lit up. As I handed him his Sour Patch Kids, my brain sensed what my heart already knew; before me was a child. Smart and compassionate and formidable, and with a maturity steeled by fire, but a child.

We perceive so much of the world now through our televisions, that we've gotten used to experiencing it in just two dimensions. We watch the stories unfold on our flat screens, and the people moving through them appear flat as well.

David Hogg and his fellow survivors are heroes to many, and villains to some. Two dimensional characters in a heartbreaking plot. But to his mom, David is just a boy. A kid who loves theater and Sour Patch Kids and being silly with his friends.

And who happens to also be changing the world.

Thanks, kids. The task should not be yours, but it is.

—————————— ★ ——————————

June 20, 2018

"And now here is my secret, a very simple secret:
It is only with the heart that one can see rightly;
What is essential is invisible to the eye."
—Antoine de Saint-Exupéry
The Little Prince

As I walked up the steps to the train platform, I heard a great deal of laughter. The station is usually quiet at this hour, the morning rush having passed and carried away it's often stoic crowd of very serious business people focused intently on what the Wall Street Journal says will guide the market that day. So, the sound of all of this talking and joy was surprising.

Upon reaching the top step, a dog greeted me. Attached to the dog was a harness and handle, and holding the handle was a young lady without sight. I had to overcome the colossal urge to reach out and cuddle this dog up, as his harness carried a sign that read, "Please don't pet me. I'm working."

The laughter I'd heard all the way from the bottom of the steps was from this group of about thirty young people, mostly kids, who can't see.

In overhearing their effervescent conversation, I learned they were awaiting the train that would whisk them to their first Broadway show.

To a person, they smiled and laughed. With gusto.

I thought of the train that had left earlier, full of quiet as people in tailored suits concentrated in silence on stocks and bonds and other "important" stuff. Not a smile to be found.

These kids, up against odds I cannot fathom, every single day, did nothing but laugh the entire time we waited.

Thanks, universe. Message received.

Sight and vision are not the same thing.

July 1, 2018

Of the new lights *Hamilton* has shone on the history of our nation, one of my favorites is the one cast on John Laurens. As Gregory D. Massey, author of a Laurens biography says,

> *Unlike all other southern political leaders of the time, he believed that blacks shared a similar nature with whites, which included a natural right to liberty. 'We have sunk the Africans & their descendants below the Standard of Humanity,' he wrote, 'and almost render'd them incapable of that Blessing which equal Heaven bestow'd upon us all.' Whereas other men considered property the basis of liberty, Laurens believed liberty that rested on the sweat of slaves was not deserving of the name. To that extent, at least, his beliefs make him our contemporary, a man worthy of more attention than the footnote he has been in most accounts of the American Revolution.*

In the show, this important aspect of who Laurens was, and what he believed, is distilled down to a single line; "We'll never be free until we end slavery."

Yorktown is one of the most powerful numbers in the show, moving inexorably with ever-increasing pace and energy toward the climax of the battle. When the white flag of surrender is flown by the British, the accelerating forward motion propelled by the dynamic choreography and gaining musical thunder finally slows, as the American soldiers take in the enormity of what has just happened. Laurens says, "Black and white soldiers wonder alike if this really means freedom," and then, in a poignant moment made more so by the fact that it comes in one of the few instances of the show when there is no other sound or movement, as the music completely stops, Washington answers into the still silence, "Not yet."

Because, as we know now, Laurens' dream of slaves being freed after the revolution would not come to pass. In fact, Lincoln's Emancipation Proclamation would not be issued for another 81 years, and slavery would not be officially abolished in America until the ratification of the 13th Amendment in 1865 (and as the newly minted large-scale awareness of Juneteenth now reminds us, the news of the ratification of that Amendment wouldn't reach Texas for another five months—two and a half years after the Emancipation Proclamation). It took twelve amendments in the "Land of the free" to finally get to the one that said, "You cannot own people." It really makes you want to go back and look at the first twelve, doesn't it? Of course, there's a loophole in the Amendment (that remains there today) allowing for slavery as "punishment for a crime." So, after the Civil War, new laws were passed, mostly in southern states, but in places like Connecticut and New York as well, known as "Black Codes," where people who were black could get arrested for things like, you know, getting married, or not remaining "quiet and orderly." Which meant it was *extremely* easy to be convicted of a crime if you were black, and again become a slave in everything but name. Then, these codes morphed into the "Jim Crow" laws, which held sway for another hundred years, and wouldn't be ended until passage of The Civil Rights Act in 1964. Almost two-hundred years after Laurens tried to end slavery, the abject misery of oppression in varying degrees would continue, the echoes and repercussions with us still for the "descendants" he presciently worried about. That is the enormity of what is contained in the two simple words Lin put in Washington's mouth; "Not yet."

America has never been fully realized. Not yet.

Once upon a time, some dreamed of a land where all would be free. In their imaginations, no queen or king would rule but the one within each chest. It would be a home where, as equals, individuals would follow their hearts, free to become, without limit, whatever they might.

If you found yourself somewhere where your becoming was thwarted, where something kept you from realizing the depth and breadth of you, you could flee in search of "America."

And were you, after your difficult passage, to find this sacred place, you'd be greeted by wide arms gathering you to their breast, saying, "You made it. You wrenched yourself from your oppressors, be they kings or poverty or despots or violence. You found the unimaginable strength required to say, 'enough,' and make your way here, to the land of the free. Which means you are one of us."

Of course, the piece of earth where this "grand experiment" would occur was taken by force. Whole cultures, largely, were nearly wiped from the face of the earth. Then, those seekers of "America" began to build—using, largely, a stolen people. The "land of the free" was constructed by many who were not.

The idea was beautiful. The thought that Hamilton and Washington and Laurens and all the rest tried to manifest was a noble one.

But . . .

It was only fifty years ago, just a fleeting, minuscule fifty years, that people of color were finally "granted" the full right to vote. In a land where nothing was meant to be granted. A place where rights were supposed to be endowed, always there, and inalienable.

Beyond our hopeful imaginations, America has never fully been. Not yet.

But, it can.

The sacred idea that is America beats within us.

"America" is not a political system, you see.

It is a human longing.

Someday, we will live up to the words, we will become the land our Mighty Woman says we are:

> *"Not like the brazen giant of Greek fame,*
> *With conquering limbs astride from land to land;*
> *Here at our sea-washed, sunset gates shall stand*
> *A mighty woman with a torch, whose flame*
> *Is the imprisoned lightning, and her name*
> *Mother of Exiles. From her beacon-hand*
> *Glows world-wide welcome; her mild eyes command*
> *The air-bridged harbor that twin cities frame.*
> *'Keep, ancient lands, your storied pomp!' cries she*
> *With silent lips. 'Give me your tired, your poor,*
> *Your huddled masses yearning to breathe free,*
> *The wretched refuse of your teeming shore.*
> *Send these, the homeless, tempest-tossed to me,*
> *I lift my lamp beside the golden door!'"*

—EMMA LAZARUS
THE NEW COLOSSUS

July 7, 2018

Tonight at *Hamilton*, a boy walked up to the bar with his mom. I'm not great with ages (except mine—I'm thirty-five, and have been for some time) but I'm guessing he was about eight. Looking into eyes that gazed at me from just barely above the top of the bar, I asked this young man if he was excited for the show.

One of the best things about the experience of working daily at *Hamilton* has been to see, up close, what Lin's show has done for live theater with kids. No movie or app or instawhatever competes with what happens on our stage. While inside the Richard Rodgers Theater, all that exists for these kids is *Hamilton*.

As you might know, theater, in general, is struggling in this country, up against a plethora of entertainment options—many of which are experienced in isolation. So, it gives me great joy to ask a kid if they are excited to see the show. Almost without fail, their eyes get wide, they often jump a little, and answer with some form of,

"ohmygodicantevenbelieveimhereivebeenwaitingforeveriknowevery singleword!"

Tonight, though, when I asked this young boy, whose skin happened to be on the darker side of the skin complexion spectrum, he said, "Pretty excited, yeah."

"Do you know all the words?" I asked.

"No," he said. "I don't know too much about it but my mom said it's really good and she made me read a book about history and she said it's all people who aren't white, so I'm excited about that!"

He said this with genuine joy.

We live in a time when, still, what you look like matters. And this innocent, beautiful little boy is growing up in a world where he mostly sees people who don't outwardly resemble him.

Throughout most of government and television and movies and theater, he is made to feel as though he is "other."

And that sucks.

Someday, we will live in a society where we are judged only on the "content of our character." When to even notice the color of someone's outermost organ (beyond, perhaps, a subconscious sense of gratitude for the gift of diversity), let alone have it influence opinion as to who they might be, will be absurd.

In the meantime, a little boy whose skin is dark got to see people who look like him singing and dancing and being awesome. When he said, "It's all people who aren't white so I'm excited about that!" I looked at his mom, and she smiled the "the things kids say" smile. I turned back to the boy and said, "I am too! All kinds of people and colors is what makes the world great!" Which widened his beaming grin more.

As Marie said after the boy and his mom left, "Representation matters."

Yes, it does.

May we soon see that there is nothing to see in someone's appearance. What is meaningful is not perceivable by the eyes.

Until then, thanks, Lin, for *Hamilton*.

---- ★ ----

July 19, 2018

I was once devastated when a girlfriend broke up with me. I thought we were in love, and that she was "the one." I stopped eating, and lost any motivation and direction I had. All I could see was my loss and all I could feel was my sadness.

My sister said, "It's terrible to see you this way. She's completely taken the wind from your sails."

And I thought, *She's not taken the wind. She's taken the sails.*

But she hadn't. The sails, you see, are you. They come here with you, and you take them when you go. They're who you are.

Sometimes, though, they get knocked down.

And sometimes we get hit so hard we think they're gone.

But we're wrong about that.

Because the sails are us. Lowered, for a moment, knocked over, even, but not gone.

Which is good news. Because the wind of hope is always blowing. That gale born of love and goodness and justice and peace and what's right. This wind is truth, and it's always there.

Always.

History records the stories of some who knew about this truth. This wind. People who, you might think, had little reason to believe it was there. People who, against insurmountable odds, as the rest of the world would have figured it, surmounted them anyway, and turned a tide of one kind or another once their sail billowed.

Because when the current of truth is captured, odds no longer apply.

This truth is perennial, it is intrinsic, it is fundamental, it *is*.

It needs only us to be located again.

So, find your sail, friends. And get ready to hoist.

We've got a current to catch.

August 7, 2018

Matthew Mccaughneyonahy (we're close, as you'll see—that's why I don't have to Google how to spell his last name), walked up to me with his family tonight. I said, "Matthew! It's me! I'm sure you remember. We met at the *Lion King* about ten years ago. You and I had a great time as you waited for someone by the bar while she went to the bathroom."

Matt (I often just call him "Matt" or, sometimes, "Matty," given our tightness) looked into my eyes and said, "Mike? Is that you???"

And my head spun. Because, in reality, we aren't quite as close as I may have let on. I was truly shocked. I thought, *Wow! Oh my gosh! I must have made a pretty big impression on him that day! Nobody slings a Junior Mint like me, apparently! Ten years later, he remembers my name!*

Then I looked down to grab a cup and saw the new name tags our company is requiring us to wear pinned to my chest.

So.

September 4, 2018

Tonight at *Hamilton*, a young boy in a *Hamilton* hat and shirt told me this was "the greatest day of his life." He was probably about nine or ten years old and there with his dad.

I asked the boy's dad if it was the greatest day of his life, too.

"Well," he said with a grin, "I'm not really into rap music."

"Dad, it's not rap music, it's just, you know . . . amazing!"

There is some "rap music" in there, but the young man didn't seem to have much use for labels, beyond "Amazing."

It was clear that his dad was not a fan of musicals, and would not ever be caught in a Broadway theater but for his kid. He said, "Well, whatever it is, I get to hang out with you, and that's all I need."

The boy smiled a smile that glows. He wasn't just agog about *Hamilton*. He was over the moon to experience it with his dad.

I thought about how, someday, many, many years from now, this will be a day this boy goes back to in his mind over and over again. (He won't remember the guy who served him his Sierra Mist, but that guy will remember him).

Theater wasn't my dad's thing, either.

He grew up in a family where abundant money wasn't a reality. The idea of taking him and his three siblings to see a play was a nice thought, but not one that could be seriously entertained on the wages my grandmother made on the line at a fabric factory, and my grandfather as a truck driver.

There also wasn't money for post-secondary education, so after high school, my dad started working right away as a driver for a small delivery company, before eventually getting the job he'd hold for the rest of his life with FedEx, spending many of those years being paid close to minimum wage.

And yet, somehow, he helped me pay for college

It's not really "somehow." I know how.

He made it possible by putting in the sort of herculean effort only a love uncommon can inspire. My dad, in all his decades of work, never, not once, took a sick day. Wanting the time-and-a-half rate, he was behind the wheel every weekend. Each Christmas, we waited late into the evening for his arrival, after the rest of the family had already eaten and exchanged gifts, when he'd finally walk in, still clad in his FedEx attire, and still smiling.

For years and years and years.

After all the work he'd done, the countless hours of his life he'd sacrificed so that I could go to school and get a job that made my life more financially comfortable than his, you can probably guess what happened when I called him, in my senior year of college, to tell him that I wanted to switch majors from science education to acting.

Acting. A "career" notorious for its lack of financial comfortableness.

You can just imagine how upset he was.

But . . . you'd be imagining it wrong.

Because when I finally worked up the courage to call my mom and dad in my senior year, and tell them I wanted to be an actor, meaning I'd need to spend a fifth year at school, which amounted to two years of my dad's pay, what he said was, "All I need is for you to be happy."

So, an actor I became.

In the immediate years following graduation, I worked at theaters around New England, and my dad never missed a show.

Not one.

Though Shakespeare wasn't his "thing," it became so as soon as the words were coming from his son's mouth, and he drove all over the Northeast to hear them.

On one occasion, though, I got a job at a theater much further away. I'd been cast in an extremely small role in *Witness for the Prosecution* at the Cincinnati Playhouse in the park, and my dad had only one possible chance to see me perform. He worked six days a week, so the only opportunity would be the Sunday matinee. However, he worked until around 5pm on Saturday, and would have to be back early on Monday. "Dad," I pleaded, "I don't even have any lines! Please, please don't worry about it!" See, my dad was afraid to fly, so the only option was to make a fourteen-hour drive from Connecticut to Cincinnati, see the show, and immediately begin the long trip back—which was obviously an insane idea. It would absolutely not be worth all that enormous trouble to see me play Security Guard 2, who stood silently for three hours. Though he and my mom had tempestuously divorced when I was about five, they eventually became close friends again (like they were when they'd met at twelve) so, when I told him she'd booked a flight and was going to spend the weekend with me, it made him feel a little better. Still, though, he was insisting on coming, until I said, "I'd just worry about you the whole time!" That finally got through to him, and he agreed to stay home "Just this once."

Imagine my surprise, then, when I looked out from my silent, stationary position that Sunday afternoon while guarding the courtroom door, to see my dad in the second row.

He'd done it.

He left work on Saturday, drove through the night, watched me stand there and say no lines, and then, smiling, got back in the car, this time with my mom, (who'd cancelled her return flight to go with him and keep him awake) for the long return trip to Connecticut to be at work the next morning.

I think about this *all the time*.

And the boy I met at *Hamilton* will think about today *all the time*.

We aren't always fully aware of the moments that will be precious. The ones we'll pull out, time and again, to feel.

Whenever I need to feel my dad, it takes only my memories to get there.

This father, tonight, thought he was taking his son to a show, but what he really did was give him a tether. A moment the boy will take out over and over again, throughout his life, any time he needs to find his way back to his dad.

Today, that tether is my most guarded possession, as eight years ago, my dad passed.

Which means he doesn't have to drive all over the place anymore to see me in shows.

Now, he flies.

———— ★ ————

September 9, 2018

"For, while the tale of how we suffer, and how we are delighted, and how we may triumph is never new, it always must be heard. There isn't any other tale to tell, it's the only light we've got in all this darkness."

—James Baldwin
Sonny's Blues

Not long ago at *Hamilton*, I walked out of my office as the show was going on, to find a woman dancing in front of one of the lobby televisions that show what is happening on stage.

"You don't want to see it live?" I asked.

"I just needed to move for a minute," she said with a big smile.

"Oh," I said.

And joined her.

So, for five seconds, this woman and I danced.

When I got back behind the bar, my friend and coworker asked, "Do you know who that is?"

"No," I responded.

"It's Serena Williams!" replied my incredulous and exasperated bar partner.

I'll admit that tennis hasn't been a sport I've followed very closely, so much so that even after being told who the woman was, though I knew her name, I wasn't fully aware of her historic place in the sport—a position I learned is already secure, but that Serena isn't finished solidifying. This weekend, my old dance partner was playing for what would have been a record tying 24th Grand Slam tournament win (and this, just one year after having a baby). The final took place in the late afternoon, so I was able to catch a good part of it between *Hamilton* performances.

On two show days, I'll often go to the same quiet restaurant during the break, but on this Saturday, the hole-in-the-wall local secret was unrecognizable—loud and boisterous and packed to the brim with people. Luckily, the bartender is a friend, and she had a seat reserved for me among the tight crowd, all gathered to watch Serena volley back and forth with an opponent nearly half her age, fighting to etch her visage even more deeply into the Mount Rushmore of tennis. The event was of such a magnitude that people sitting around me who knew less than I did about tennis had been taken in by the match. I was informed, by the way, that it's called a "match" by a polite woman beside me, after I'd noted what a good "game" it had been. What I haven't figured out is the scoring system, which remains a complete mystery to me. Why the points are inexplicably "love," 15, 30, and 40 (I mean, come on—not only do they increase by different intervals, but one of those is a word) instead of 1,2,3,4 has yet to penetrate my dense brain.

Things in the match took a quick turn against Serena after being treated in what many feel was an unfair way—a way a white male tennis player likely would not have been treated. She lost points for arguing with the white male line judge, and ultimately lost the US Open. The gathered crowd around me loudly voiced displeasure, feeling as though the chance at history had been taken from Serena, and speculating that racism and sexism might be at the root of why it happened. It was clear the majority of those sitting in the stadium in Flushing, Queens were having a similar angry reaction, vociferously airing their unhappiness with the calls to deduct points, as the dispute between Serena and the line judge went on. It was very uncomfortable to watch the entire scene unfold, and I can't imagine how tough it was for the joy-filled woman I'd danced with in the lobby, now fighting back tears as the world looked on.

"Tough," of course, is relative. It's not the tough Serena's ancestors survived. It's not the tough where life and death and dignity hang in the balance. It's not the thousands of years of tough her gender has endured. But though it might sometimes be less obvious, sexism and racism maintain their tenacious and ugly grip on American society. And in some ways, they are more insidious than in the past. In times earlier, they wore white hoods and proudly designated bathrooms and buses and burial places. They made women certain of the kitchens they were "made to be in" and the voting booths they were not.

The issues our great-great-grandparents dealt with have changed clothes since then. Garbed now, in better camouflage, they can at times be more difficult to discern. Today, they are largely found in paychecks and rates of imprisonment and differences in opportunity and things one might more easily miss than a sign displayed above a water fountain. But the differing disguises make these thieves of equality and dignity no less institutional, persistent, and hurtful.

And we felt we were watching them hurt Serena right now, on live television.

When the announcer, standing on stage with Serena and Naomi, attempted to begin the trophy presentation ceremony, the crowd booed so loudly that he had trouble proceeding. He paused to let the assembled masses continue their vocal assault, all seemingly outraged at the outcome, incensed by the, perhaps, underlying sexism and racism. Serena's young opponent (who had just become the first Japanese player in history to win a Grand Slam) wept and covered her face, overwhelmed by the intense emotion coming from the nearly ten thousand people surrounding her. Serena, noticing the tears streaming from her opponent's eyes, gathered her in her arms and joked, trying to wrench a smile from the 20-year-old girl, on the world's stage for the first time. In what should have been a moment of great joy and celebration of accomplishment, the young lady silently cried, pulling her visor down over her eyes. And Serena, being the woman she is, would have none of that. So, when the microphone was placed in front of her and the audience stopped booing for the first time, at first giving an enormous ovation, and then quieting to listen, in a moment filled with love supreme and class we don't deserve, Serena put aside the painful unfairness she'd been subject to, and said to the crowd, "This is her first Grand Slam. I know you guys were here rooting for me . . . but let's make this the best moment we can. Let's give credit where credit is due, and let's not boo anymore. We're gonna get through this, and let's be positive." With a big smile she said, "Congratulations Naomi! No more booing." The crowd acknowledged their love for Serena and her message, and, as she'd requested, stopped booing.

And then, just to make sure I was good and emotional there at the bar with my new friends, already surreptitiously crying into my plate of baked Brussels sprouts, it was Naomi's turn to address the crowd. Standing beside her idol, the hero of hers that she'd watched when a little girl from the upper levels of the stadium she now stood at the center of, and whom she'd just vanquished, Naomi said to Serena, through streaming tears, sad herself about how things had gone, "I know that everyone was cheering for Serena, and I'm really sorry it had to end like this." At which point, she again got choked up, unable to speak. So the crowd, which had been following Serena's instructions to no longer boo, instead remaining subdued, instinctually erupted in enthusiastic applause, understanding this young lady had been paying a price she'd done nothing to deserve, that she'd been unsuspectingly caught up in something much larger than this moment.

They seemed to, at once, realize she was an innocent piece in a puzzle spanning hundreds of years, a puzzle being built in ways over which she had no control, and that this piece involving her, being placed right then, was one of the lurching fits and starts cultures take as they move toward justice and egalitarianism. Unprepared for the weight of this internationally televised cultural growing pain, she'd been overcome.

So, they applauded their hearts out.

The camera panned around the stadium, featuring face after face clapping for all they were worth, with not many dry eyes in the house. Feeling the new support, Naomi continued, "It was always my dream to play Serena in the US Open Finals." She then turned towards her hero, and in the middle of this immense, painful, complex thing said, so simply, "Thank you for playing with me."

"*With* me," she said.

Something about that phrasing just did me in.

Not *against*, but *with*.

Well, my Brussels sprouts needed the extra salt anyway.

Sometimes tennis is a lot more than tennis.

September 16, 2018

Let me tell you something about a guy who was a big part of my childhood, and who I've had very mixed feelings about—Roger Clemens can be a really, really nice guy. I met him last night at *Hamilton*, and with a nostalgic smile told him I was a lifelong Red Sox fan, and that when I was a kid he was my favorite player. My childhood hero. When he left the Red Sox to join the Blue Jays, I was beside myself, and when two years later he became a member of the archrival Yankees, well my little heart just broke. "So, my feelings about you are complicated," I told him. He laughed and said, "I understand, man. I totally understand. I'm just always glad to meet someone who loves baseball." And that I do. Because of my dad.

"Are we rooting for those guys?" ask I, at maybe five years old, pointing to a guy in a pinstriped uniform on the television.

"No," says my dad, "they win all the time. It would be easy to root for them. We're rooting for the other guys."

The other guys were the Red Sox. The team that *never* won. Until Roger Clemens came along.

Watching Clemens peer so confidently over his glove, and strike people out at rates rarely seen with a fastball that left his hand at super human speeds, was thrilling. I became an instant devotee of the "church of baseball," as the film Bull Durham would soon term it. I watched whenever I could, and sometimes snuck out of bed to check the scores, just so I could call my dad the next morning and say, "How about that game!" My parents had gotten divorced, so with those phone calls, baseball became something more than baseball between my dad and me.

On a midsummer morning when I was eight years old, my dad surprised me with our first trip to Fenway Park in Boston. I knew the stadium so well from watching the games on TV that being outside of it, and looking way up at the towering lights above the Green Monster, Fenway's famed outfield wall, was surreal. But upon entering the park, I realized something was wrong with our television. Stepping out of the tunnel that led to our seats, suddenly, the whole of the field revealed itself, as my breath caught in my throat. What I'd seen on the small screen in our living room did not prepare me for this. And the love I had for baseball instantly swelled. I had no idea grass this bright and green and perfect existed. The moment overwhelmed my senses and I stopped us in our tracks to take it in. I squeezed my dad's hand. "This is amazing," I stammered. "Yeah," he agreed, and lifted me up on his shoulders to get a better look.

We'd gotten there early to watch batting practice, so the stadium was mostly empty, allowing us to get right near the field. Soon we heard a periodic "pop" reverberate around the park, which meant it was time for my dad to reveal another surprise—he'd gotten us tickets for a game that "Rocket" Roger Clemens was pitching. As he got loose in the bullpen, the sound we now heard was his fastball hitting the catcher's glove. We made our way over to the bullpen area, and from just above in the bleachers we watched Roger warm up. I couldn't believe we were this close to him. Again I looked up at my dad. "This is amazing."

The stands eventually filled with fans and we found our seats. Roger came running out of the dugout and took his place on the mound. The home plate umpire issued a loud and exhilarating "Play ball!" and Clemens lifted his glove in front of his face so that his eyes were just visible above it, as I'd watched him do so many times before. This was certainly *the best day of my life*, I thought.

In between Fenway Franks and ice cream and peanuts, I peppered my dad with question after question. With a patience I now find hard to imagine, he answered each, and taught me the rules to the game. And something soon became clear: when he answered me, he wasn't just talking about baseball. As young as I was, I quickly realized this was an avenue for him to communicate to me what he'd found to be true and of value in life. He was using sports to teach me not how to be a player, but a person. He was teaching me about fair play and justice and losing with grace and winning with humility and always trying your best and what it means to be a "good sport" while you do all of it.

The Red Sox got way behind, and Clemens was taken out of the game. And then, they got further behind. By the sixth inning of the nine-inning game, people began to leave, and when the last inning rolled around, the park was nearly empty. "Where is everyone going?" I wondered aloud. My dad said that since the Red Sox were losing by so much, and a win seemed unlikely, people were exiting early to avoid the traffic. "Are we going to leave?" I asked.

"Do you want to?"

"No," I said.

"Good," he responded. "Because I'm having fun here with you. And there are still three outs to go. We can't give up. You never know."

The Red Sox lost that game. By a ton. When the final out was recorded, he looked at me and rustled my hair and said with a joy that made me believe him, "We'll get 'em next time." And as we drove home, laughing the whole way and reminiscing about everything we'd seen, I suddenly realized why my dad didn't mind rooting for a team that hadn't won a World Series since way before he was born. I think I knew it all along, but it became starkly clear that day: for my dad, it wasn't about winning. It was about playing the game, and how you do it. It was about trying your best and staying for the whole thing and keeping the faith—and having a light heart about you while you do it.

So, after that idyllic summer afternoon, I loved the game with a new depth. And I loved how my dad loved sharing it with me. And how Roger Clemens and the Red Sox had become "ours."

I was pining for the day to arrive that I'd be old enough to play myself. As much fun as my father and I had watching the sport, it thrilled me every time I imagined him seeing me out there on the field. Over and over I would daydream about hitting the winning home run while he sat in the stands, and how proud it would make him when my teammates lifted me on their shoulders and carried me triumphantly off the field. I imagined him jumping for joy, yelling "That's my son! That's my son!" While all those around patted him on the back, the way, I imagined, those around Roger Clemens' dad did with every win.

There is a song written by Craig Carnelia included in the musical review *Diamonds* that goes like this:

> *It's the bottom of the ninth. There is one man on, and two men out, and the score is four to three. There's a man at first, and a man at bat, and the man at bat is me. I'm kinda scared, and I'm kinda small, and I'm stronger than I seem. And I take a swing, and my dad is there, and it's what you'd call a dream . . . .*

This was on my mind when my first official practice arrived. The memory of this day is one of the indelible ones for me. One of those recollections we have that can be pulled up in stark detail, instantly back in the sights and sounds and smells and feelings, no matter how many years ago they were written to or within (or however it works) the neurons of our brains.

I am nine years old, and I walk up to the plate wielding a bat far bigger than me. The nerves I'd been feeling all day now crescendoed, as squarely upon my small shoulders the spotlight fell. It was the first practice for Criscola's Service Station, my little league baseball team, and all day long we'd been working on hitting. One by one my teammates had taken their thirty swings, I think it was, while the parents cheered and jeered from the bleachers. I was taken aback by how some of the fathers, in particular, had acted. "Keep your eye on the ball! Keep the bat up! Pay attention!"

Wow, I thought, *these dads are not messing around.* It was something of a competition, it seemed to me, as if their child's ability (or lack thereof) said something important about them as parents.

"Keep your head in the game!"

But it didn't feel much like a game. This was serious stuff. And now, it was my turn. I hit my cleats with the too big bat, and knock off the dirt, just like in the big leagues. I step into the box, raise the bat over my shoulder, and await the pitch, ready to give it my best Jim Rice try. The coach winds up, lets the ball go, and I see it coming towards me. When it gets close enough, I take a swing, and my dad is there, and it's what you'd call a nightmare.

On the heels of the fifth "swing-and-a-miss," a horrifying realization dawned on me; I couldn't hit. At all. I was worse than the Red Sox. As my thirty swings piled up, the weight of the shame tripling with each painfully silent swing of the bat, as ball after ball sailed safely past, people began to laugh. And not only the other kids. I clearly remember a coach chuckling behind me. Eventually kids in the outfield sat down, bored even with making fun of me. But the worst part wasn't the embarrassment I felt about not being able to put the bat on the ball, it was knowing that my father, my poor father, was sitting in and amongst all those other dads that had been shouting all day. I couldn't imagine how ashamed he must have been as each ball drifted completely out of any danger whatsoever into the catcher's glove. *He must have run away,* I thought. The black-and-white photos of him playing baseball in high school that had been published in the local newspaper flashed in my mind. My grandmother had shown me the articles with his name in them with such pride. She read the caption under a photo of my dad playing football, frozen in time as he is heroically breaking the tackles of three opposing players—no match, were they, for him. "Bob Anthony breaks away during yesterday's game to help the Mayors win their fourth straight," it said. I was sorry my dad would never get to brag about me in this way, his face alight as he reads a caption to my kids.

Mercifully, my coach finally said "Next!" as I finished flailing impotently about in the batter's box, wanting to cry, kids now lying down in the field, but that would have just been the ultimate icing on the cake and those laughing jerks would have just loved it and I can't stand them I hate baseball I hate the Red Sox they always lose and so do I . . . and then, I catch a glimpse of my dad. I instantly look back down, remembering he must be wishing I wasn't his at that moment, and not wanting to give him away to the other dads, because maybe he was pretending some other, better kid belonged to him . . . and as I'm looking down I think of the face of the man I just saw. *Wait. That couldn't have been my father. The man I just saw was . . . smiling. Certainly my dad would not be smiling at an awful time like this. What could there possibly be to smile about? I had likely just embarrassed him out of loving me*, I thought. But it sure looked like him. So, I glance again, and sure enough, not only did my dad not run away, but he is right there, in those stands, right there in the middle of all those other dads, and he is smiling at me.

After practice, I began the painful walk towards him, still able to hear kids and parents discussing my nearly incomprehensible lack of ability—"Don't worry, we'll bat him last." And I am devastated. Making my dad proud on the field was not going to happen. I get over to the stands, looking at the ground, and my dad puts his hand on my shoulder, takes off my hat and rustles my hair and with a great big grin says, quite simply, "We'll get 'em next time." And we went to get ice cream. And he let me ride in the front seat . . . after opening the door for me, with everyone able to see. I was his son, and he wanted them to know.

That weekend, I asked my dad if we could go to the park and practice. Though I certainly entertained the notion of giving up and never going to that awful place again, I somewhere knew that might be disappointing to him. It seemed he couldn't care less whether or not I hit the ball, but I felt he hoped I was brave enough to keep trying. At my insistence, he pitched to me for hours, as we attempted to troubleshoot the problem. For most of the day, I would swing and miss, and we would laugh . . . an altogether different laugh. It appeared at some point that I was just not going to be able to do it. But that didn't matter. This was fun. As twilight approached, both of us tired, we'd tried and laughed so hard, my dad said, "Try putting your front foot back a little, and straighten up a bit." And I did. He pitched the ball, and I saw it and swung at it and . . . BANG. Ohmygosh. I did it! I had finally hit a baseball. Something about the new stance allowed me to see the ball better, and my eyes and hands were suddenly talking. With that small adjustment, I was now making contact on every swing. This, of course, meant my poor dad had to continue pitching to me until the sun went down— which he smilingly did, having as good a time as each ball went over his head as he had been when each was ending up at the backstop.

At the next practice, when it came my turn to hit, I heard someone ask the coach if perhaps they should skip me. To save me the embarrassment. One of the assistant coaches on the team was a family friend, and he said to me, "Don't worry, even your hero Roger Clemens can't hit! Maybe you were meant to be a pitcher like him." But I walked up to the plate, looking over at my dad with a "here-goes-nothin'" shrug, and took my new stance. The pitch comes, and I take a swing, and after a solid "crack," silence filled the field.

I hit that ball farther than anyone had ever hit a ball, I was sure.

Ball after ball soared out over the heads of my teammates. And I steal a look at my dad, sitting there once again in the midst of those other dads who are now cheering for me. But not him. He is not cheering. He looks *exactly* as he did when I was not hitting the ball. While other parents applauded and yelled "great swing!" and "that's how you do it!" my dad sat there in silence and smiled his quiet smile. Not a word from he. Just that smile that says it is not whether you win or lose or hit the ball, it is, indeed, how you play the game.

The night a child of mine is born, and I contemplate the weighty charge of guiding a life, I will kneel by my bed and pray but one prayer; "Like father, like son."

And whenever I'm wondering what to do, how to be a dad, I will go and ask the man who lives in my memory. I can always find him. He is always there. He sits in my bleachers, and always, he smiles.

I love you, Dad. I wish you'd been there when I met Roger Clemens.

So I could have introduced him to my hero.

---★---

October 30, 2018

Friends—Jessica Biel is here, and I'm pretty sure we just fell head over heels in love with each other. She smiled right at me. Well, not *right* at me. You never smile right at your crush. Obviously. That would be too overt. She smiled at a guy next to a woman who was beside a guy who was standing near my bar. Methinks that makes it pretty clear.

And she hasn't even seen me dance yet.

So, I'm sorry Justin Timberlake.

★

Update: after intermission I went back to speak with Jessica Biel (Jessie, I call her) and lay it all out on the line. I said, "I just want you to not worry that you'd have to be alone if things didn't work out with what's his name. I'm prepared to wait two years for you."

She said, "Oh wow. Hmm. Do you think you could give me three?"

I thought about it for a moment and said, "Yes. Yes, I can do that."

She responded, "Thank you so much. And *Hamilton* will definitely still be running by then, so I'll know where to find you, Mike."

And I gasped.

I really have not gotten used to wearing this name tag.

★

November 9, 2018

> *"'But it isn't easy,' said Pooh. 'Because Poetry and Hums aren't things which you get, they're things which get you. And all you can do is to go where they can find you.'"*
>
> —A.A. Milne
> *The House at Pooh Corner*

Last night at *Hamilton*, our pal Gregory Treco was on in the role of Burr, and we listened as he sang "The Room Where It Happens." Gregory's voice is ridiculously good, and all of the bartenders stood in the lobby commenting on it. And it reminded me of something.

One evening after work, some friends and I went out for a coworker's birthday party. We landed at a place called Joe's, which had karaoke that night. Having had a drink or two more than my body and brain were capable of fully dealing with, I decided to sing a song—very, very poorly. The tune I chose was "Scenes from an Italian Restaurant," by Billy Joel. Unfortunately for those in attendance, it's a long song—a really, really long song. The stage was near the entrance, and about halfway through the horror I'd been putting my friends and the bar's other patrons through, the door swung open and a man and woman entered. Slightly intoxicated, I put my arm around the shoulders of the guy and placed the mic in front of his lips, asking him to sing along with me. When I did this, the crowd erupted in hoots and applause—it seemed they were thoroughly enjoying my invitation to this stranger to join in, and being a good sport, he acquiesced. When the next verse started, as he swayed in time with the inebriate who'd commandeered him, his voice took me by surprise. It was *stunningly* good. Caught so off guard by the dulcet tones, in fact, for a moment I actually stopped singing and just stared at him with big, drunken eyes. When the song ended, the people in the bar went absolutely wild, and I thanked him for rescuing me.

Returning to my seat, the birthday girl said, "Oh my god! I can't believe you did that!"

"What do you mean?" I asked.

As it happened, the man I'd thrown my arm around was a guy named Lance Bass, who was a member of a fairly well-known group called NSYNC, and everyone in the bar, except me, it seemed, was aware of that.

I've long wanted to be in musicals. For as far back as I can remember, I'd wished that I could sing the way Lance Bass is able to sing—so powerfully and movingly and, seemingly, effortlessly. But, for whatever reason, my vocal cords don't vibrate the way his do. They don't make the beautiful sounds others create. The kind of sound that Gregory's and Lance's make.

So, instead of being in Broadway musicals, I've made a life working in their lobbies. I serve drinks and snacks and ask people to "Enjoy the show," of which I am not a part. The show my physical apparatus is not good enough to give them.

And here's what I've discovered; the joy I got from doing karaoke that night with my friends in a small bar is the same joy Lance Bass gets from singing on stage in front of 20,000 people. Joy is not relative. Joy is joy.

When your parents tell you that you can be whatever you want to be, they aren't telling the truth. They are doing their parental duty, but they aren't telling the truth.

What they could say, and not worry that they are being dishonest, is that you can be as happy as you want to be.

As the Stones observed, though "you can't always get what you want . . . you can get what you need."

Which is happiness.

And happiness is not relegated to the physically or mentally or emotionally gifted. It comes from all sorts of places. No talent required.

———————— ★ ·—·——

November 12, 2018

> "*If forever*
> *does exist, please*
> *let it be you . . .*"
> —A.R. ASHER

Every once in a while, I come out from behind the bar at *Hamilton* to do some acting (I'm not entirely certain how the show survives without me, but somehow, they get it done). One of my favorite places to work is a theater I've been lucky enough to perform in many times over the years, located in an idyllic Maine town called Monmouth. So all-encompassing is the "can this be real?" feeling of the neighborly New England quaintness of Monmouth, that it can be easy to think the iconic play *Our Town* wrote itself. (It didn't. I tried writing a play during my offstage time there once, and I was more successful the first time I "skied" not far from the same town, when I slipped off of the "J bar" lift, just managed to grab the bar before sliding away down the mountain, and instead was dragged up it face first while the skies that were supposed to easily unlock if I fell down—so the instructor had told me—instead hit me in the head the whole way up. Once atop the slope, exhausted from the trip up, instead of trying to ski down, I slid all the way on my butt. And that whole thing went better than my first attempt at a play. So no, *Our Town* didn't write itself, and I apologize to Thornton Wilder for ever thinking it might have).

Being in Maine is always such a lovely time. There's nothing like getting out of the big city for a while to slow and quiet things down, enough sometimes to even hear your soul a bit. In fact, every time I return to Maine, I wonder why I ever left. Then I wake up with a spider on my face, and I remember.

Truly, though, I love being here. And to be here for an acting job makes it all the more wonderful.

We had the day off from rehearsal today, so I went to the "best breakfast place in town," according to the gentleman sitting beside me at the breakfast bar at Denny's. As we chatted, I noticed two men, both, I'd guess, in their late eighties, talking and smiling. Every now and again, one man would touch the other's hand. After a while it became clear they were a couple. From their accents (their beautiful accents, my Maine friends), I could tell that they had lived in the area for years, and were probably born here. I thought about what life must have been like for these two men, growing up in a small town, finding each other in it, and falling in love. Then, somewhere along the line, realizing a good number of people (the government included) did not consider their love to be deserving of the same sacrosanct respect as the love found between people of the opposite sex.

Today, though, none of that seemed to matter to them.

When it was time to leave, one went to retrieve a wheelchair. His husband (judging from their wedding bands) was much weaker than he. The stronger of the two returned, and ever so gently lifted the man he loved up from the seat. He pulled a jacket from behind the chair and helped his partner get it on. The man's arm got stuck, and he said, "I'm sorry, I can't do it," then made some remark to the younger couple sitting in the next booth about the difficulties of "getting old." The more able man said, "It's okay, it's okay," and he slowly made his way to the other side of his husband to guide his arm through the sleeve. Once he had him seated in the wheelchair, he struggled himself to bend down, then moved the footrests into place. With the tenderness you might employ while handling a fledgling bird, he placed the feet of the love of his life, whose knees were clearly in pain, on the rests. The whole process took a good five minutes. He then went to grab his own cane from the booth, came back, and with his hand on his husband's shoulder said with a big smile, "We did it!" They and the younger couple laughed together for a moment, as they ever so slowly made their way out. And if you were to look at all of that today and see anything but a love that made your eyes leak, well . . . you've got to get some better glasses.

Because love is, indeed, Love.

And that's that.

---★---

December 19, 2018

"To know even one life has breathed easier because you have lived, this is to have succeeded."

—BESSIE A. STANLEY /
ALBERT EDWARD WIGGAM

Today at *Hamilton* a young boy, maybe five or, like, twelve (I really can't tell how old kids are) came up to the bar before the show with a woman I assumed was his mom. She asked him if he wanted a soda, to which he said, "That's probably a lot of money."

"Don't worry about that, dude," she said, in a way that made me think this wasn't her son. It was more of a cool aunt vibe I was getting. It's the way I imagine my sisters would be with my imaginary children.

I asked this shy five or twelve-year-old boy if he was excited for the show.

"I'm *really* excited," he said.

And I figured that would be all. Unexpectedly, though, he continued, "I'm in a bit of a transition right now. I live in Florida, but me and my mom have to move to Colorado." He then reached up and put his arm around the woman's shoulder, saying, "My amazing aunt made everything easier by surprising me with this show."

So, then she got teary-eyed.

So, then I did (just for a second!)

I don't know what this boy's story is. We never know what someone's story is, often including our own. Unless you happen to be Gandhi or Rumi or some other "self-actualized" being, most of the time we are mysteries even to ourselves. But what wasn't a mystery was that this kid has a good aunt. And that she and the show Lin put into the world somehow made his life a little easier.

We're all in this crazy thing together, pals.

———————— ★ ————————

January 6, 2019

Tonight at *Hamilton*, I met another Make-A-Wish Kid and her mom.

She was asked what she'd most like to do in all the world, and what she said was, "I want to see *Hamilton*."

Being a human sure ain't for the faint of heart.

In my imagination, the universe is full of destinations souls can choose. Some places, in my imagination, are full of nothing but joy.

But some are more trying.

It's like choosing your college curriculum. The lessons, whatever it is they are, need to be learned. And there are many ways to get the learning done. You might take an easier course load, spread out, spending more time to finish than one who chooses to cram in the extra class on Friday mornings at 8am.

And in my imagination, Earth is one of the more difficult schools.

It's a place a soul comes to only if it's a very hearty soul—a soul full of spirit, as it were. An adventurous soul. In my imagination, when we're all hanging around wherever it is we are when we're not here or in some other schoolroom, we talk to each other about where we've been, and where we're headed. And in my imagination, when a soul tells her companion over "other place" coffee that she has decided to come to Earth, her companion puts down her cup, and sighs in admiration.

Not many, in my imagination, are cut out for Earth. Not many have that kind of courage.

So very few, I am certain, have hearts big and brave enough for a course like this. And without question, there are but a tiny number of hearts that glow as bright as that of the little girl I met tonight, or her mom's.

In my imagination, on the other side, this seven-or-so-year-old shines so brilliantly it's difficult to look directly at her. If our human eyes were set up in such a way that allowed us to see who someone was, this woman and her daughter would be suns.

The child has a brain tumor. I don't know what the prognosis is. I have no idea how much time on this side she will spend. I know only that her older brother and her mom and dad put on brave faces today, as her wish, a wish to see people sing and dance and pretend on a stage, was granted.

In our play, in this one, here on earth, I wonder if this girl and her mom and brother and dad know they are playing heroes?

Has she, from her tiny wheelchair, any idea how powerfully she has affected our plot—how profoundly she touched me and everyone in that theater lobby today, and who knows how many more?

I doubt it.

But I know that I just met a brilliant light. And in my imagination, before she and her mom came here, over coffee, their fellow souls' jaws dropped when they told them the level of difficulty they'd chosen this next time around. In collective admiration they sighed and smiled and thought, "I hope, someday, to be just half as brave and beautiful as they. Oh my."

When I asked the girl's mom if she minded sharing what her daughter was struggling with, and she told me that she had a brain tumor, and it has now paralyzed her, as tears welled in her eyes, I could only get out, "She will be in my heart."

To which she said, with such deep earnestness and gratitude, "Thank you."

The thanks, of course, is to her and her daughter. To know such love and courage and bravery exist is to know that anything is possible.

Today, in my imagination, I met an angel.

But I don't think it *was* my imagination. The more I consider it, the more I feel that angels are real, and that I just met one.

And the next time we meet, wherever that may be, the coffee is on me.

Post Script—The assistant company manager, Holli Campbell, wrote this to me after reading this post: "If you're talking about the same girl I think you're talking about, there's another detail to this story in particular that I think makes for another really heartwarming moment. This girl wasn't even here because of the Make-A-Wish foundation. Don't get me wrong; we do a ton of work with them and they're always fantastic. But Scarlett and her family actually came to us because one of her classmate's parents learned that it was her dream to see Hamilton but knew it would be an unnecessary financial burden on the family. So, he got in touch with us and purchased 4 tickets, which he gifted to the family. We see a lot of negativity in the world, but it's these acts of human kindness that remind me why we're here."

———————★———————

January 16, 2019

"For the reason of laughter, since laughter is surely
The surest touch of genius in creation.
Would you ever have thought of it, I ask you,
If you had been making man, stuffing him full
Of such hopping greeds and passions that he has
To blow himself to pieces as often as he
Conveniently can manage it- would it also
Have occurred to you to make him burst himself
With such a phenomenon as cachinnation?
That same laughter, madam, is an irrelevancy
Which almost amounts to revelation."
—CHRISTOPHER FRY
THE LADY'S NOT FOR BURNING

I've long believed that humor, true humor—the sort that comes at no one's expense, the kind that binds strangers so quickly together by highlighting our common folly—is a form of fundamental truth born in some other "dimension" or "realm" or other word describing this place science hasn't pinned down, which sometimes leaks into our existence, and inspires us to keep reaching.

I was once fortunate enough to meet a woman who could hear the leak.

In 2007, Carol Channing spent a day with my MFA class in Detroit. In the photo on the following page, she had just read something I'd written, and laughed. And that sound was the sweetest I'd ever heard. It rang not in my ears, but in my soul, and I'll never forget it.

Hamilton, and all of Broadway, just dimmed their lights in honor of Carol.

In a time when women struggled in so many ways, even more so than now for basic equality, Carol was no match for the societal tide against which she swam, breaking through all kinds of barriers. She did it with a courage and joy uncommon, and mostly, she did it with that other place humor.

A gift like hers, offering a glimpse of that place, comes but once in a lifetime—if we're lucky.

Godspeed, you wondrous lady.

---★---

January 24, 2019

Today on the train platform, a man walked up to me as I was reading a book and said, "I'm so sorry, I don't mean to interrupt . . . I just had to tell you that I LOVE *Hamilton!*"

And I thought, *Oh, well, gosh! Somehow he recognizes me!!! How??? Does he follow me on Facebook? Did he watch the PBS documentary EXTREMELY closely? Either way, I am going to make this guy's day when I offer him not only an autograph, but also a selfie. No charge! I'll even sign his face, if he'd like. It's not easy being a celebrity, but this is what we sign up for.*

At which time he said, "I saw the *Hamilton* logo on your bag, and realized you were an even bigger fan than me!"

Oh. Let me just put this sharpie away.

---★---

February 3, 2019

First, a confession: I'm a bit of a nerd. I read books (that I can't actually grasp) about quantum mechanics and how we think the universe works. I follow professors of string theory on Twitter. I once took a trip to Columbia University, just so I could go to the physics department and touch the door of Dr. Brian Greene's office.

Things like that.

Well, one day at *Hamilton*, I thought I saw Michio Kaku.

Dr. Kaku is a brilliant theoretical physicist. He's appeared in a bunch of documentaries and television shows and writes exhilarating books about the mind-bending aspects of reality we are starting to discover. He's one of the scientists, like Bill Nye, who have penetrated the thick walls scientific complexity builds between truth and people to enter the public's awareness. I became so aquiver when I saw him that I left the bar (to my customer's dismay) and sort of started to, well . . . chase him. You could say I actually chased him down the hallway as he made his way into the theater. But I couldn't help it! I was positively flustered, my heart beating wildly at the prospect of meeting this man in person. But, as the lights flashed and people rushed to find their seats, I lost him.

I ran back to the lobby and found my friend Tim (who is the best house manager on Broadway) and started to hurriedly tell him and the man he was speaking with about who I thought was there. As I was breathlessly explaining this theoretical physicist sighting, I realized the other man I was speaking to, who was looking at me rather oddly, was Tom Brady.

You know, the Super Bowl Tom Brady from the New England Patriots.

It literally went like this; "Kaku! He's here! Right now! This guy is working on stuff Einstein never got to finish—what he knows about the quantum realm is just oh my gosh you're Tom Brady."

And Tom laughed and said, "I am, yeah."

Please consider this from Tom's perspective; A flustered, sort of sweaty man runs up to him (one of the most well-known people in the world right now) and pantingly begins to ramble about quantum mechanics and unified field theories and anti-gravity. I will never forget his priceless look of confusion.

After I'd more properly explained myself, I asked, "How many times has someone not noticed you because they were distracted by a theoretical physicist?"

"Haha, yeah," he said with a smile. "I think that's a first."

Tonight is the Super Bowl, and the Patriots are in it once again. Good luck, Tom—try to utilize what we discussed regarding aerodynamics and probability waves, and all should be well.

———————— ★ ————————

February 6, 2019

"There are more things in heaven and earth, Horatio, than are dreamt of in your philosophy."

—WILLIAM SHAKESPEARE
HAMLET

Skyler, a good friend of mine, is working with me at *Hamilton* this week. He's not only a great guy, but a smarty-pants on top of it. He listens with patience as I go on about the "other-worldly" experiences I've had over the last years, but always tries to keep me grounded with explanations that don't shatter centuries of scientific "truth." However, sometimes I think a fracture is made in his citadel of logic, and questions flutter in. When David Blaine inexplicably performed the magic show for just the two of us, for instance, I was certain I noticed some soft spots appear in those "all can be explained" fortifications. And when the *Hamilton* lobby recently became giddy at the presence of a visitor, those cracks widened more.

For the first years of *Hamilton's* Broadway run, the lobby staff was often abuzz with news of a celebrity we were expecting. If someone is very well-known, we generally have them come in early and secret them away to avoid a stir while getting the rest of the thirteen-hundred people seated in twenty minutes, which means we often have an opportunity for a brief greeting before the doors open to the public.

At this point we're used to this, and it takes quite a lot to bring back that pre-show ballyhoo. Even Beyoncé caused only the slightest departure from the norm (except for Marie, who became incapacitated with ardor, and just sort of lay on the floor in a fetal position). One day, however, that ebullient commotion did return, though surprisingly, a celebrity had nothing to do with it.

See, immediately after my dad passed, I started to see monarch butterflies quite often. It became a sign for me that my dad was still here in some way, guiding the wings of these metamorphosed beings, I imagined, into my sight to let me know that he'd, too, left his earth-bound caterpillarness and become something else.

My deeply broken heart, of course, was surely now taking in and transforming what had always been—I wasn't suddenly seeing more monarch butterflies, I was suddenly noticing them. Any rationalist, like Skyler (and me, for that matter) would clearly perceive it that way. No matter the odd times and places the butterflies showed up, the skeptic would insist they had been there all along, but I'd ascribed no particular significance to them until now.

So, when heading back to work on the first day since the funeral, feeling utterly broken and lost, and thinking only of my dad, I saw a monarch butterfly fluttering about down in the subway track (which is the only place I could possibly have seen it, my despair having cast my eyes at my feet), I thought first, "*Dad?*" but quickly regained my scientific wits and recategorized it as the coincidence science says it absolutely must be, my ever-skeptical brain bringing me back to earth like a caterpillar woken while dreaming of wings.

Over the following months, though, I and my family would have many more seemingly significant monarch butterfly encounters—all of which were profound and healing for us, but useless to science, and eventually, at least for me, occasionally dulled in mystical wattage by endless rationalizing.

But then . . .

Unable to let my dad go, not willing to allow his dissolution into the ether, I started to research the various lines of evidence out there suggesting the possibility that life goes on after death. There seemed to be many, as it turned out. But, no matter the strength of the evidence, always there was a powerful, intelligent, and joy-sucking retort.

For each crack in the veil separating this world from my dad, a skeptic would be there to cement over the breach. Often, these skeptics were highly educated and well-spoken and offered unquestionably erudite answers for why my dad was surely gone.

Not least among these skeptics is a man named Penn Jillette. You've probably heard of him—he is half the duo making up the magic team of Penn and Teller. Penn, no doubt, is smart and talented. And with his partner, is capable of performing tricks you'd be forgiven for imagining might portend the existence of actual magic. But Penn is quite clear that there is no such thing as magic. He goes to great lengths to let his audience know that nothing "paranormal" exists in the universe. He takes extreme, angry exception to those who might try to make you think otherwise. And not long after my dad's passing, and the new-to-me frequency of butterflies, here was Penn performing his act in one of our theaters. I watched as, on the first night, he and Teller did a bit they call "The Psychic

Comedian," where they pull off spectacular feats of "mind-reading." Penn took great pains, though, to make clear that there was absolutely no mind-reading involved. His point was that if he, a magician with no "paranormal abilities" whatsoever, can perform this trick, then, with practice, anyone can.

He focused in on people who claim they can hear or see or somehow feel our deceased loved-ones—people who call themselves "mediums." People like the one my family met with, who delivered a message she claimed was from my dad, that I was certain could only have come from him, a message which acted like a rope thrown into my pit of despair.

Penn said that these people were using the same techniques he employed, combined with unscrupulousness, and our grief and desperate desire to believe, to dupe us for money. And at the back of the theater, there I stood, simultaneously astounded by the "mind-reading" trick he'd performed, and devastated that it might mean the woman who'd called herself a medium and claimed to hear a message (that only I knew) from my dad, was a fraud.

The trick was amazing, and I determined I needed to go back to see it again, hoping to discover something of the method. So, the next night, I stepped back into the theater just as the bit was beginning. Penn opens the illusion by saying, "Let me be clear; there is no such thing as the paranormal. Anyone who claims to have the ability to speak to your dead loved-ones is a liar. Everything they say is (pardon, but I'm quoting) BULLSHIT." As my spirit sank upon hearing this utterance, my rational mind beginning to believe the words he spoke, my eye was drawn to a movement above the magician.

The Marquis Theater is located within the Marquis Hotel on Broadway. It is on the second floor of the structure, and you need to go through one set of doors, up an escalator, through another set of doors to reach the theater lobby, and finally a last set to enter the house where the stage is. And somehow, in the midst of Times Square, up the escalator and through three sets of doors, as the word "bullshit" landed heavy on my heart, above the orchestra-level audience a butterfly fluttered into the light.

My heart leapt—I'd worked on Broadway for a decade, and never had I seen a butterfly inside a theater. And lest I believe it was just the wishful imagining of a desperately broken heart, so big was this winged creature that others within the audience noticed it. A murmur and wave of enjoyment went through the crowd as my little miracle darted this way and that. In the instant Penn told the audience that nothing communicates past death, my dad, above the very head of the man issuing those words, seemed to tell me otherwise.

(If only Penn knew his very speech *against* seemed to me to be used in a powerful *for*, and would keep me headed forward on the path I still travel).

But the story doesn't end there.

Not long after, I was back at *Hamilton* in the Richard Rodgers Theater. While we were getting the bar ready, I recounted to Marie the story of the butterfly appearing over Penn's head, and together we wondered aloud what the chances of such a thing might be.

Like me, Marie has worked on Broadway for quite a long time, and as we stood behind the bar getting it set up, I asked, "Have *you* ever seen a butterfly in a Broadway theater?" To which she said, "No, I haven't. Not once."

And as I began to respond, "I know it sounds insane, but I really feel like it's some sort of message from my dad," out of the corner of my eye I saw a flutter. We turned to look, and sure enough . . . well, you know. Zig-zagging past was, indeed, a butterfly, and soon everyone in the lobby was enjoying the unusual and mesmerizing sight.

Much of the house staff has grown up on Broadway, and over all of the combined years, no one I spoke to remembered a butterfly entering a theater, including Darnell, an usher, and Kendra, who works for the merchandise company. In these pictures, you can see the look of incredulity on Darnell's face, and the bewilderment on Kendra's as they look up at the butterfly, which had perched herself within one of the lobby chandeliers.

They were surprised simply at its presence, having no knowledge that Marie and I had just been discussing the possible "paranormal" meaning behind the appearance of a butterfly in a Broadway theater at an instant that seemed profoundly significant, right when *this* butterfly appeared.

I know my friend, Skyler, would like to chalk all of this up to coincidence. I know he thinks that a butterfly is just a butterfly.

But I suspect he feels, too, beyond what he might like to admit, that it may, sometimes, also be more.

---★---

February 11, 2019

"Cold in my professions, warm in my friendships, I wish, my Dear Laurens, it might be in my power, by action rather than words, to convince you that I love you. I shall only tell you that 'till you bade us Adieu, I hardly knew the value you had taught my heart to set upon you."

—ALEXANDER HAMILTON
A LETTER TO JOHN LAURENS

One of the finest scenes ever filmed is in the movie *Waking Ned Devine*. In it, an old man gives a eulogy for his best friend, who happens to be, through a marvelous set of plot twists, sitting in the front row. This is what he said:

> *Michael O'Sullivan was my great friend. But I don't ever remember telling him that. The words that are spoken at a funeral are spoken too late for the man who's dead. What a wonderful thing it would be to visit your own funeral. To sit at the front. To hear what was said. Maybe to say a few things yourself. Michael and I grew old together. But at times, when we laughed, we grew younger. If he were here now, if he could hear what I say, I would congratulate him on being a great man. And thank him for being a friend.*

I've got a friend who never waited to tell you how much you meant to him.

I've got a friend who thought of you any time he went somewhere, and brought you things you'd forgotten you'd ever told him you liked. Like mangos. And crab cakes.

Small things. Ridiculously meaningful, big thought small things.

I've got a friend who hugged me every time he saw me. A real hug. Not the flimsy-pat-softly-on-my-back-kind. The *real* kind. The kind that makes you know he loves you, and wants you to feel good.

I've got a friend who made every room he walked into a better one. A friend who tried, every single time he saw you, to lift you up.

Every. Single. Time.

I've got a friend named Rasik Ohal.

But Rasik didn't have the same kind of friend in me. Darn it. Gosh darn it. Though I can't blame myself, too much, I suppose, for that. Because no one has the energy to be that good of a friend, all of the time.

Nobody does.

Except . . . Rasik did.

Somehow, Rasik did.

In a recent social media post, he mentioned his favorite quote, from *MASH*:

"Do you guys really think you can change the world?"

"Nope. Just our little corner of it!"

He then wrote, "I hope in some small way I've been able to make your corner of the world a little better. You've certainly done that for me."

From up there, Rasik, I hope you can see how many corners you bettered. How many lives you eased.

I know we haven't lost you. I know you are here now, and always will be. But filling the gap left by your physical departure . . . we sure need someone like you at a time like this. Someone to bring us the softest tissues he could find, because it's okay to cry, but he wouldn't want any noses getting sore. Someone to tell us a joke, even a bad one, because it's never too soon to laugh again. Someone to wrap us in that six-foot-something frame with an unmistakably healing bear hug when that laugh turns again into tears.

What a way to spend a life. Using all of your time just walking around, brightening things. Lightening things.

I'm sorry it took so long for me to say this, but I'd like to congratulate you on being a great man.

And thank you for being my friend.

Rasik worked with us at *Hamilton*, and Gregory Treco (who Rasik deeply touched—as he did everyone he met) has vowed that his performance of Burr on the 17th (which happens to be the day of Rasik's memorial service) will be dedicated entirely to him. One of the finest voices on the planet, sending off one of the finest people.

Flights of angels, you beautiful being.

---★---

February 14, 2019

"I wish you knew how much of you there is in everything I do.
It can be the smallest thing . . . trivial . . . mundane . . . but you're
there. Under the surface of it somewhere.
I wish you knew how I carry you with me always . . .
everywhere I go."

—RANATA SUZUKI

If I miss the first train home, while I wait for the next one, I'll often stop in at a bar for a glass of wine (you know, for the flavonoids).

Tonight, there was a man playing guitar and singing. And he was great! At the end of the first tune I was there for, I was about to applaud, but no one else did. People were involved in their conversations or phones or both, and seemed to take no notice of the man pouring out his soul through song.

He beautifully played another which ended in the same silent fashion. I looked right at him and gave him the "thumbs up," hoping to relay my appreciation, albeit silently.

But then, for whatever reason, Rasik came to my mind.

As I sipped my Chardonnay (a drink he insisted on buying me the very last time I saw him, for my birthday—even though my birthday had been two weeks earlier) I wondered, *Had Rasik been sitting here beside me, what would he do?*

And the answer was obvious—Rasik would have clapped with gusto. A person had just put himself out there and sung us a song, and there is simply *no way* Rasik would have let that go without giving that person a loud and heartfelt acknowledgement (and probably buying him some of his favorite fruit).

So, as the echoes of the third song fell away, and that same silence started to fill the room, I raised my arms above my head, and applauded with everything I had.

For Rasik.

And, wouldn't you know it, Rasik had the entire bar joining in within seconds. The man playing the guitar looked up with some surprise saying, "Wow, thank you. Thanks everybody. That's . . . wow."

He thanked everybody, not knowing there was actually just one person to thank. One person who happens to not be in a physical body anymore.

We are all so deeply connected. In the ultimate truth, really, we are one, and we have a choice in every moment, about how we affect the whole. The decisions we make do not have walls. They ripple out into the rest, and alter it.

Try to make your decisions in such a way that someday, when you are no longer physically here, a person in a previously uncaring bar will suddenly feel appreciated, because even though you aren't physically here, your actions—who you were—is.

Your ripples go on forever. Make them well.

Like Rasik.

February 24, 2019

As Marie made a woman her drinks, she asked if she was excited to see the show.

"Yes!" She responded. "This is my fourth time, actually. Which is pretty significant, because when *Hamilton* first opened in August of 2015, I was told at the box office that no tickets were available until April. That wasn't great for me, because I had only been given until March to live. But I bought the tickets anyway, and hoped. And every time I see the show, I continue to prove that doctors don't know everything. So, yeah, I'm excited!"

Science is far from knowing everything, friends.

There is magic on the *Hamilton* stage.

But science can't quantify it, so to science, it isn't real. And yet, I watch it every day.

There's magic in you, too.

It won't show up on an X-ray or MRI, but it's there.

Believe, mostly, in that.

———————★———————

April 2, 2019

That was awkward.

I just met Patrick Mahomes, and, oh my, it was awkward.

Even though Broadway shows are full of some of the most athletically gifted people in the world, musical theater and sports often aren't thought of as going together. Lin has used the term "sportsball" on occasion, referring to the fact that sports aren't his thing, and making the joke that he doesn't know enough about them to discern the difference. Another friend of mine, a fantastic actor who, like Lin, isn't big on sports, puts it this way; "Whenever a game is on, I root for the clock."

Such is the popularity of *Hamilton*, though, that it easily bridges whatever perceived gap there might be between the two "worlds." In fact, it's a frequent occurrence for me to look up and see famous athletes.

Patrick Mahomes is a young quarterback in the NFL, and an absolute phenomenon. He can do things on the football field seldom before seen. Such an enormous star is he, in fact, that even my pal Andy, who isn't entirely clear on the difference between a touchdown and a home run, recognized him.

As he came up to me during the second act, he could somehow tell I knew who he was (I think possibly because I said, "Oh my gosh, Patrick Mahomes!") and he reached out to shake my hand.

And that's where it all went south.

Patrick was going for one of the cool handshakes, and I was going for the classic style. So, I tried to readjust to him, while he simultaneously tried to readjust to me.

Which meant we ended up just sort of awkwardly rubbing/bumping/slapping hands or something. It was some terrible, jumbled mash up of handshake styles that lasted for what I'm certain was five minutes.

It was awful.

Red-faced, I handed him his drinks and said, "It's on me. Just please don't ever speak of what happened here tonight."

Someone, I beg you—teach me how to cool shake. *Please.* For all of our sakes.

June 2, 2019

> *"It is difficult*
> *to get the news from poems*
> *yet men die miserably every day*
> *for lack*
> *of what is found there."*
> —WILLIAM CARLOS WILLIAMS
> ASPHODEL, THAT GREENY FLOWER

Today, as Pride month begins, someone set alight the rainbow flags outside of a gay bar here in New York City, sending them up in flames before cowardly exiting the scene.

The story made the news.

Tonight, at *Hamilton*, a young couple, both female, with small rainbow flags painted on their cheeks, who had come "All the way from Tennessee!" told me how grateful they were to finally be at the show, having waited "for years," and how blissful it was for them to be "somewhere where we can do this!"

And then they kissed.

Right there in the lobby, these two young ladies, making it clear that wherever they live, those folks still have some growing to do, marveled at the fact that they could give each other an outward show of their inward feelings, and get only smiles in response.

You probably didn't see this moment on the news.

No cameras were summoned when the older lady behind these two girls offered to pay for their drinks. No reporter appeared when they then kissed again, lost in each other's eyes, as the same lady and her mate smiled behind them.

The world will never hear about the love I saw expressed today, while the person who burned those flags, operating out of some sort of deep-seated and subconscious self-hatred and fear, got all the press.

New flags will fly tomorrow. The act was a temporary, fleeting expression of a person not yet, you know . . . okay.

The kiss, though, the love between these two young people (who happen to currently inhabit physical bodies of the same sex) is not fleeting.

The news usually covers the aberrations. The stuff that stands out.

Love doesn't stand out.

Because it's everywhere.

And today, while a misguided individual took out his pain on a symbol of love, *actual* love made itself beautifully known in the *Hamilton* lobby.

Keep the faith, pals.

The real news isn't on the news.

The Hamilton stage awash in the colors of the rainbow
for light check in honor of Pride

★

June 13, 2019

"The best portion of a good man's life is his little nameless unre-membered acts of kindness and of love."

—WILLIAM WORDSWORTH

TINTERN ABBEY

About two years ago, in between shows on a double day, the producers provided lunch for the cast, crew and house staff, which they do on occasion if, for some reason, the break isn't as long as usual, and time is tight. As I ate my food from behind the bar, a man came over and put his plate down near mine. "Mind if I eat here?" he asked.

"Of course not!" I said.

The man introduced himself as Eddy, and asked what I did for the show. Answering this question always makes me feel a bit insecure, embarrassed, I suppose, to be a 40-something-year-old concessionaire working around all of these people who have trained so hard to do what they do. But when I said to Eddy, "I'm the bar manager," his face lit up with what looked like genuine delight as he exclaimed, "Oh wow! That's so cool! That's awesome!"

I don't know if "cool" is the way I think of it. I didn't have to work an untold number of hours, as the actors and crew involved in the show did, to hone my skills. Selling Kit Kats and soda comes surprisingly easy. In fact, you might not be able to tell the difference between someone selling their first Kit Kat, and someone selling their one-thousandth. But you can definitely tell the difference between someone doing their first pirouette and someone doing their one-thou-sandth, or singing their first note compared to their millionth. Eddy, though, truly wanted me to feel like what I did was "Awesome."

When I asked what he did, Eddy said, "I'm a new swing for the show." This meant he'd be learning multiple ensemble tracks, ready to go on as an understudy if someone got hurt or needed a day off.

Being a swing on Broadway has got to be one of the toughest jobs in the world. The amount of information you need to hold in your head and body is preposter-ous to someone like me, who can barely recall where the orange juice button is on the register screen. But someone who swings is required to learn and be able to perform at a moment's notice, the unbelievably intricate steps an ensemble member makes throughout an entire show. And not just one ensemble track, but maybe two or three or four! The work involved is just extraordinary. And yet, to be a swing is to have your heroic efforts often go unsung.

Tonight, Eddy came up to me with an enormous smile upon his face. "On Sunday, I go on as Hamilton," he beamed.

When we met, he told me about his family, and his sister who is a world class doctor. He said that being the first male Asian-American to be cast in *Hamilton* was amazing, but his sister was "the real star in the family," saving lives as she does on a daily basis.

When Eddy takes the stage as Hamilton on Sunday, no doubt his mom and dad will be overcome with pride at what their kids have accomplished. But if I get the chance to talk with his parents, what I'm going to tell them about is how accomplished Eddy made me.

You can practice a pirouette until it's perfect. But the ability, and desire, to make someone else feel good . . . well, that comes from somewhere else.

And his mom and dad should know.

Break a leg, Eddy.

---★---

June 29, 2019

"Thousands of geniuses live and die undiscovered - either by themselves or by others."

—MARK TWAIN

Tonight at *Hamilton*, I met a mom who brought her daughter to the show as a gift for her high school graduation.

After her daughter and son took their sodas and snacks and ran up the steps to the mezzanine, their mom laughed and said, "Oh okay, I see, you take your stuff, that I bought, and you're done with me!" They all laughed, as her kids continued on their way. She then confided in me, "This is a special day. I didn't know if she'd make it. She's had some learning difficulties, but she never let it stop her. The day she learned how to multiply two times two was the proudest day of my life. Until she turned into such a nice kid—such a nice person. Now, every day is the proudest day of my life. She thinks we're here because she graduated from high school, but really we're here because she's her."

And, pals, it just really hit me right in the heart!

It made me think of my dad. There was a day when I was in sixth grade and got into a "fight." A high school kid had been picking on my friend on the bus. My friend was heavier than average, and this kid just wouldn't leave him alone, talking loudly about his weight in hurtful ways. Finally, I stood up and said something to him. I don't remember what it was. I just recall that whatever I said prompted him to get up from his seat and come over to us, and then slap me, hard, in the face. The driver stopped the bus to come back and break up the "fight," and then, I guess, reported it, because the next day, my dad asked me what happened, at first upset that I'd fought with someone. But when I explained it to him, rather than ground me, he said, "Want to get some ice cream?"

Much later my dad would tell me how proud of me he was for what happened that day. I was a small kid, and my slight body could not come close to "cashing the checks" my heart often wrote. But my dad said, "No matter how big or not we are, trying to do the right thing is all that matters. Whether or not you do it isn't the thing. Just that you wanted to. And that you tried."

For some people, multiplying two by two is nothing at all. There is no effort involved. But for some, enormous effort is involved. And what ultimately matters isn't that you get the right answer, but that you wanted to.

When I first met Lin Manuel Miranda's parents, I asked, "When did you realize your son was a genius?" Lin's dad was hesitant to use that word, but he did offer, "From very early we knew he was special." And I said, "Special??? He's an actual genius. In fact, whenever I speak with him, I think (and this is totally true) I wonder how many sentences I can get out before he realizes I am not a genius?"

But, here's what I truly believe; we've all got genius.

"Genius" is the thing that makes you vibrate. It's the reason you came. It's the thing that makes you most alive.

The girl tonight whose mom was euphoric at her graduation may not be great with math, but there's no doubt she's a genius at something. Like making her mom glow, for instance. Who cares if you can multiply if you make your mom light up like that?

I'll tell you what I think my genius might be; it's the tendency to notice and be moved more often by what's good than by what isn't yet.

There is something in all of us that puts us in tune with our deepest selves, and the universe. It may not be obvious. It may not be the usual stuff we associate with "smart." But it's the only smart that matters.

What's your genius?

July 2, 2019

Tonight at *Hamilton*, a man pre-ordered a drink from me. In this case, they pay for it right then, and it's waiting for them at intermission behind a little card on which we write their name.

When this very nice guy gave me his name this evening, I couldn't help but smile and repeat it to him with what he thought was confusion. Assuming I wasn't familiar with it, he spelled it out for me, letter by letter. What he had no way of knowing is that I was not confused, but astonished; he'd just said the same rather uncommon (at least to me) name that a dear friend of mine had.

As I finished writing the letters down I decided to tell the man that his name was meaningful to me, but when I raised my head he'd already stepped away, and the next customer stood in his place. I looked back at the card, momentarily frozen as I calculated the odds. I then showed Marie the name I'd just written. Marie also halted what she was doing, similarly shocked, and feeling as though this might be a quick "Hello" from our friend.

I glanced up towards the ceiling, gave our pal a wink, and continued serving. And that was that.

I thought.

Intermissions at *Hamilton* are rather frantic. Thirteen-hundred people squeeze into the too small lobby, jockeying for position in both the bathroom and bar lines. Amidst the frenetic pace of our bartending duties, it took a full five minutes for me to notice a man patiently waiting at the end of the bar where people pick up their pre-orders. When I finally became aware of him and suddenly saw that it was the man with the same name as our friend, I said as I poured another customer's soda, "Sorry, I didn't see you. Did you need something else?" At which he silently waved his hand, gently asking me to come closer. When I got to him, the buzz of intermission fell away, as though this man and I were suddenly in our own little bubble. "No," he said. "I don't need anything. I just wanted to let you know that I actually bought this for you, and your friend," as he nodded towards Marie.

In my fourteen years bartending for Broadway shows, this has never happened. Not once.

No one, in all those years, has bought Marie or me a drink.

I hurriedly told her what was happening as he smiled and waved to us and softly said while walking away, "Have a very great night," before disappearing into the sea of people.

If you knew my friend, if you'd had the great pleasure and honor of having spent any time at all with him, you'd know this is *exactly* the kind of thing he'd do.

I don't know anything about anything, friends. I don't know what it all means or how it all works or what is going on.

All I do know is this:

My friend just bought me a drink.

July 5, 2019

"And when I meet Thomas Jefferson, I'm 'a compel him to include women in the sequel."

When I was a little kid, I went to Space Camp. I and my friend Eddie and a bunch of other kids.

All boys.

It wasn't that girls couldn't go to Space Camp. They surely could. But not many did. And we don't need to go far back into history to understand why. In fact, considered within the scope of the known human story, the days depicted by Don Draper and Mad Men are within the blink of an eye to today.

When I was a kid and went to Space Camp, I was told every day on television that what I was meant to play with were G.I. Joe "action figures," toys that glorified war, while my sister was told she wanted to make muffins in an Easy Bake Oven.

If you wanted something else, if she preferred to play with my G.I. Joe, and I decided to use her Easy Bake Oven, or even, goodness forbid, play with her Barbie doll (not Barbie "action figure") well, that was just weird.

That's where we were. In the evolution of our consciousness, that's just where we were.

And here's where we are today, less than a blink of an eye from when I went to Space Camp, and TV told my sister her desire was to bake: when I asked the young lady in this photo if she wanted to be an actress and one day perform in *Hamilton*, she said, quite simply, "Nope. I'm going to be an astronaut."

July 15, 2019

"Muddy water, let stand, becomes clear."

—Lao Tzu

I locked myself out of my house today.

See, my new car that "Will never break down" is in the shop this week. The dealership that told me my new car would never break down was nice enough to give me a free loaner car while they fix the things that broke down on my car that will never break down. The fixes aren't for free, but it was really nice of them to loan me a free car while they make the fixes.

So, my house keys and my car keys aren't on the same ring, as they usually are. Today, I took the car keys, closed the front door, and suddenly realized I'd forgotten the house keys. Worse, I hadn't taken my phone; I was on a trip to get ice cream—because Mondays, like all the rest of the days, are perfect ice cream days—and I didn't plan to be away long, so I left it behind. I'd wanted it to be just me and my ice cream. No outside distractions. But that meant that now I was locked out and unable to let anyone know. It was suddenly 1998 for me. And I couldn't remember what people did in 1998 when they got locked out.

So, the first thing I did was to stand there, staring at the door for about five minutes.

That didn't work.

Then I went downstairs to get into my garage where I thought I kept a spare key. But I couldn't remember the code to get the garage door opener to open the door.

I then checked all the windows to see if any were left open, but none were. For a moment I considered breaking one, as the heat began to cloud my judgement, and an ice cream cone felt worth the money it would take to replace it, but couldn't find a good way to do it.

Defeated, exhausted, and drenched in sweat, I went back to the front door and sat on the stoop, as, I suppose, would also have been the only option in 1998, and leaned against the door.

Which swung open against my weight, as I fell into the house.

As I lay on my living room floor looking up at the ceiling, my two cats glaring at me wondering what this human fool was up to now, I remembered that my door doesn't lock automatically. You can't forget the keys and be locked out at the same time, since you need the keys to lock the door.

Oh yeah, I very sagaciously thought.

After the whole debacle, I got my "largest large you have please" ice cream, returned to the house, and sat on my back deck.

It was rather windy, with occasional quite strong gusts. At one point, a bird took off from a yard behind my house, headed for a big tree that overhangs mine. Halfway through her journey, one of those gusts began to pick up. For a moment, she struggled to overcome the gust, her wings flapping faster and harder. She started to actually get blown backwards. But right then, at the moment she sensed her battle with the wind was a losing one, she stopped flapping, and coasted on the current. Immediately, she hung still in space, no longer being pushed backwards by the gust. Instead, she rode it, hovering where she was.

Once it passed, she flapped again, making it to the tree she'd been headed for.

And I thought, *Whoa.*

Obviously, given the above story about being "locked out" of my house, I'm not smart enough to get it, but it felt like the universe was trying to give me one of the most profound lessons of my entire life, all in an event that lasted less than thirty-seconds.

I don't know what it is, and am putting this out there in the hopes that maybe one of you will.

I do know, though, that more favorable winds are always on the way, and if we spent most of our energy on those . . .

Well, that tree isn't so far away.

July 25, 2019

"One child, one teacher, one book, one pen can change the world."
—MALALA YOUSAFZAI

"Education is not the filling of a pot but the lighting of a fire."
—W.B. YEATS

If teachers were paid what they are worth, Mr. Corby, a beloved high school history teacher in New Jersey, would surely have seen *Hamilton* by now. He wouldn't have had to play the *Hamilton* lottery—every single day for four years—in the long-shot hope of getting affordable tickets.

Students who were freshman when he began his quest are now, four years later, graduating seniors in his history class.

They knew how much their teacher, a person who has devoted his life to their (and our) future, desperately wanted to be in the room where it happens. They knew that for four long years he'd been listening to the tales of others who'd had the good fortune to see *Hamilton*, living vicariously through their stories, while he continued, every morning, to enter the lottery before heading to school to change their lives.

Tickets to *Hamilton* are expensive if you are a public-school teacher.

They are even more expensive, though, if you are a high school student and work after school and all summer long at a minimum wage job while you try to save for college.

Buying tickets to *Hamilton* on minimum wage takes an awful lot of time and effort. You'd have to be incredibly motivated to work that hard, for that long.

Which is why Mr. Corby was thoroughly shocked when he opened a card his history class handed him at the end of the school year, containing not one, but two tickets to *Hamilton* on Broadway for he and his wife.

See, they love Mr. Corby.

After all, he's been their tour guide to new worlds. He's expanded their sense of time and space and shown them their wondrously mysterious place in the story. He has sparked their imaginations, lightened their hearts, counseled them through tough teenage times, and helped show them where those times fit in the grand tapestry of human being-ness.

The video of Mr. Corby's emotional response to this most unlikely end to his four-year quest for tickets went viral and was eventually picked up by the major news outlets.

One of his students wrote to me, wanting to share just how much she loved Mr. Corby. She said that giving him these tickets was the absolute least they could do for a person who has given so much to them.

So, I tracked down Mr. Corby, and told him to make sure he found me. I wanted to thank him, too, and do whatever I could to make his visit special—like give him whatever he wanted from the bar, and set him up to go backstage after the show and meet with some of the cast—all of whom had a Mr. Corby.

Which is why they are where they are.

Mr. Corby, it was an honor, sir, to shake your hand.

If we paid teachers what they are worth . . . if the world honored and spent as much money on the Mr. Corby's as we do on our militaries . . . well, we might not need such vast militaries.

Well done, kids.

———————————— ★ ————————————

July 28, 2019

When a mom and her two children came up to the bar today, I asked the kids if they were ready for the show. The little boy said, "Oh my gosh. I have been waiting for this my WHOLE LIFE."

The show has been running for four years, and this boy was maybe eight. So, he was about half right. His sister, who I think was a year or so younger than he, then teasingly and joyously added, "He started crying as soon as we came in!"

"I did!" the boy said, "and I'm not embarrassed either. I can't help it. My heart is bursting right now."

Their mom chimed in to tell me, "They don't just know all the words, they *feel* all the words."

As they were leaving, the little girl came right up to me and quietly said, so her brother couldn't hear, and with a deep sincerity she trusted me with, "My heart is actually bursting, too."

We're gonna make it, pals.

Lots of bursting, beautiful hearts are on the way.

———— ★ ————

August 4, 2019

Tonight at *Hamilton*, two super big dudes came up to the bar. Now, to be clear, given my size, most people are "super big dudes" relative to me. But these guys would be big even compared to regularly big, big people.

"Wow," I jokingly said. "Did you two meet on a football team or something?"

"We did!" the mass of humanity most directly in front of me responded. "We were D1 offensive linemen in college."

D1, for those of you not as athletically inclined or interested as me and these guys are, means "division one," the highest level of college sports.

They were in their forties, so it's been quite a while since they trod the gridiron together.

"How neat!" I exuberantly and so unfootbally said. "So you guys have known each other for a long time."

"Yeah," one guy responded, "more than twenty years. Our wives brought us to this thing, so they owe us."

"Big time," his friend added.

"This thing" was a duty they were performing. Something they'd get paid back for the next time they wanted to do something their wives did not.

The thing is, though, you almost never know what's inside a person. And sometimes, they don't know yet, either.

We often accept the part we think others want us to play. If you are born with DNA that makes you grow to 6' 7" and 300 pounds, and you become an offensive lineman, some subconscious part of you might sense that people anticipate you to be a certain way. To not let them down, you might unconsciously begin to live up to what you subconsciously perceive they expect.

You can observe this within yourself if you pay very close attention.

You might notice that you become a version of you depending on who steps into the room. Much of the time we live our lives adjusting, moment to moment, to who we think people think we are. Perhaps this is why authenticity is prized and maybe rare, and why, of Shakespeare's 120,000 lines, "This above all: to thine own self be true" is probably one that you can most easily recall.

Because it can be hard to be you. To let down all defenses, and "be true."

But you're always in there, somewhere.

Something like *Hamilton* tends to pierce through the fabrications we become. Something as real and raw and true as this show helps us feel . . . us.

So, I wasn't all that surprised when, tonight, the larger of the "D1" offensive linemen came back to the bar at intermission with eyes that were pink.

"How's the show?" I asked.

"Dude," he said.

I waited for more.

"Dude," he repeated.

And, once more, after another pause, "Dude."

That's all he said.

Three "Dudes."

And I knew what he meant.

Sometimes, something reaches us. Reaches the real us—the us we don't have to work at to be. The us that takes no effort. *Hamilton* does this a lot. At *Hamilton*, 6'7" D1 football players and eight-year-old children whose hearts are "bursting" and kids who are there for Make-A-Wish are all the same. They are all people sitting there in the dark, being, just for a time, who they actually are, without the world's expectations attached.

These guys tonight were dragged to "this thing."

And then this thing showed them themselves.

Which means they owe their wives.

Big time.

August 6, 2019

Tonight at *Hamilton*, during a quiet moment right after Hamilton was shot, chaos reigned when a motorcycle outside backfired quite loudly. The show was immediately stopped as people began running in every direction, including onto the stage, looking for any exit, afraid for their lives.

This is the America we live in.

This is where the choices we've made have gotten us.

Today in America, if a loud sound is heard, we think first not thunder or accident or some other jarring but innocent thing. We think immediately . . . gunfire. Random, hundreds of rounds per second gunfire headed indiscriminately in every direction, with only one intent; to kill as many people as possible.

Last year, we had a mom who lost a child at Sandy Hook. Every time another mass shooting happens (such as the two this week) she starts getting calls from media outlets asking for comment. Not long after the Parkland shooting, and needing a break from the crush of media contacting her, she came to see *Hamilton*. She wanted to spend a night around creativity and spirit and joy and love.

The right to bear arms was, of course, enshrined in the Constitution by the people portrayed on our stage. At that time, the founders felt, from experience, that the way to keep a country free was for the government to fear the people. It made sense, at that time, to have "well-regulated" militias.

That was well over two hundred years ago. When the arms people possessed were single-shot muskets that took a half minute to reload.

If the mom we welcomed last year could travel back in time and describe to the drafters what she has been through, the way her child, along with nineteen others, was lost while sitting in a school, learning about them, surely they'd be more careful with the wording of the Second Amendment.

Today, the actors who portray the founders in *Hamilton* had to stop the show due to a future their namesakes could not have foreseen, and so did not hold in their minds when fashioning the Constitution.

Here's the thing, though; it doesn't matter that the founders did not foresee this particular outcome. What matters is why they started America in the first place.

They started America because they could no longer tolerate the world they lived in. At that moment. Right then.

So, they gathered all the courage they had, to stand up to the empire and make a new world.

A better one.

And so powerful and grand was their courage that, two hundred years later, a young genius felt compelled to write a musical about it.

It's time again, pals, to gather our courage.

See, America is not a place.

America is an idea. It's the idea that we can, together, always make things better.

The chance is always there to live so grandly, so courageously, and with such majesty that, two hundred years from now, a young genius will write a hit musical about what we did.

The founders are not the only ones capable of founding.

August 22, 2019

Tonight at *Hamilton*, I asked a very vibrant young girl, "Is this the best show you've ever seen?"

As you may have noticed, I often ask this if a kid comes up, clearly out of their mind and sometimes literally jumping with joy, as was this young lady tonight.

Usually, the very quick reply is a resounding "YES!!!"

Surprisingly, though, this girl tonight stopped jumping in place when I posed the question, and didn't immediately answer. Instead, she put her finger on her lips for a moment, considering my question, and wanting, it seemed, to reply in as honest a way as possible. This wasn't small talk, I quickly discovered, not for this young lady. Someone had asked her a question, and her big, beautiful heart, barely fitting in her little body, wanted to answer with truth. To her, the query deserved respect, and she would not reply without giving it its just due.

Finally, after I'd had time to pour her apple juice and make her mom and dad their drinks, she removed her finger from its thoughtful position upon her chin and said, "Well, I'm not sure. What matters is, I love this show."

Sometimes, if it just isn't getting through your thick skull, the universe will slap you upside the head using the borrowed guise of a little human.

While I tried, with my question, to create some sort of competition, where some things are "best" and others, therefore, aren't, these three feet of seven-year-old-but-so-much-older wisdom revealed, oh so gently, my folly: "The best" is for little brains.

Big hearts, like this girl's, know that all that matters, is that it matters.

Thanks, universe.

★

August 27, 2019

"Courage mounteth with occasion."
—WILLIAM SHAKESPEARE
KING JOHN

In the middle of intermission, Rudy Giuliani came up to the bar. It was busy, as always, and we had quite a line. Rudy and his security person walked right up to Marie, cutting the people already waiting. Marie—lovely, sweet, gentle Marie—looked at him for a moment, then at me, then back to her customer—and continued to make that customer's drink. When she finished with that person, she took the one behind her. Then, the next customer. And the next and the next and next. Eventually, Giuliani gave up, and walked away.

See, Marie is one of the kindest people I know. And no matter how much she disagrees with someone, when they are standing there in front of her, they suddenly aren't the cartoonish villain we see on TV. In that moment, when they are a foot away looking into her eyes, they're just a person, with grandkids waiting nearby. And in that moment, when someone as kind as Marie is involved, it is very difficult for her to be anything other than a decent human being towards them. At the same time, though, Marie did not want any part in normalizing Mr. Giuliani or the administration he so often speaks for, as images from our border of weeping children fill front pages. So, she did all that her goodness would allow in that moment, which was to not serve a man who'd cut the line before the people who'd gotten there ahead of him were served.

Eventually, when the line was gone and the second act was about to begin, Giuliani came back to Marie (whose dad, by the way, immigrated to America from Nicaragua, and is now a doctor who has spent a lifetime helping people heal). Though the joy that normally exudes from her might have been dimmed, Marie made his drinks with care and treated him with decency.

The fabric of the world is made in every moment, with every interaction. I could not be more proud of Marie, or the stitch she added, with a quiet, beautiful, deep dignity, to our quilt tonight.

---★---

August 28, 2019

Today at *Hamilton*, a young girl, who is blind, was led into the lobby by her family, who had not yet told her where they were going. When her mom finally said, "We're at *Hamilton*!" the girl immediately began to weep, knees going weak, as she fell into her mom's arms, sobbing uncontrollably with joy.

So, you know, I'm done for the day.

---★---

August 30, 2019

When I was a little kid, I dreamed that I'd one day have a baseball card. In my imagination, the jersey I wore in the picture would read "Red Sox." But not even in my wildest of dreams was something as profound and beautiful and important as *"Hamilton"* emblazoned, instead, on my chest.

Photos by Robyn Roth-Moise

---★---

September 1, 2019

Not to be outdone by the dancers on our team, right after this photo was taken, I went directly into a full split.

(Sadly, no pictures are available of that, as the photographer got distracted by my screams).

★

September 8, 2019

"Kilgore Trout once wrote a short story which was a dialogue between two pieces of yeast. They were discussing the possible purposes of life as they ate sugar and suffocated in their own excrement. Because of their limited intelligence, they never came close to guessing that they were making champagne."

—KURT VONNEGUT
BREAKFAST OF CHAMPIONS

A friend came to see *Hamilton* today.

Afterwards, her eyes pink and wet with tears, I asked what she thought. Haltingly she stammered, "Oh, my gosh. It's just . . . it's sort of comforting . . . to know . . . that it's always been this hard. To be, you know . . . an American. And, just . . . alive."

Yes, indeed.

What she meant, I think, is that America, the idea that is America, has always been a challenge. From the founding portrayed in *Hamilton*, to the maintaining we've been engaged in since, and very desperately fighting for now.

But just being alive, just being a person, is the really tough thing.

To her, it was a comfort to learn that a heart as great as Hamilton's did wrong and hurt people . . . even those he desperately loved.

It was healing for her to discover that a mind as grand as his made mistakes. Big ones.

Because no amount of heart or genius makes being alive any easier.

The "grand experiment" that is America goes on, pals.

And the grand experiment of being a person does, too.

September 18, 2019

Tonight at *Hamilton*, towards the end of intermission, a woman and I were happily talking about how much she loves the show, when she suddenly stopped and became quite serious as she looked at the straw she had in one hand, and the soda I'd just poured for her in the other.

"I'm sorry," she said, with what felt like embarrassment.

"I was in an accident last year, and it caused brain damage. I . . . I don't know what to do with the straw. I can't remember . . . how do I . . . ?"

I gently took the straw from her, removed the wrapper, and placed it through the hole in her souvenir cup.

"Thank you," she sheepishly said.

Right then, Act Two started and her eyes lit up. "Sorry," she said, apologizing for quickly cutting off our conversation.

"I have to run . . . this show just makes my heart swell."

And off she went as quickly as her also damaged legs would take her.

She couldn't miss a second of *Hamilton*.

Because, luckily friends, it seems the most important stuff isn't kept in our brains.

September 26, 2019

"*And above all, watch with glittering eyes the whole world around you because the greatest secrets are always hidden in the most unlikely places.*"

—ROALD DAHL
THE MINPINS

Tonight after work I went to a place called Don't Tell Mama. It's a piano bar, where mostly show tunes are played.

This evening, I sat beside a guy who didn't seem to be entirely comfortable when a group of men came in dressed in what we might typically refer to as "women's clothing," complete with heels.

This guy was in New York for the first time, here with his wife celebrating their 30th anniversary, which I discovered when his "other half" left to find the bathroom, and I took the opportunity to strike up a conversation.

"I'm not from here," he eventually said.

"We grew up being taught certain things, and New York isn't those things."

We chatted about what he meant by that for a few moments, and it was clear this man and I weren't going to be on the same page. He was kind about it, though, almost apologizing for the things he'd "been taught."

At this bar, a live pianist plays and sings songs, and now and again, a bartender or server will pick up a microphone and do a number themselves.

Tonight, the man tickling the ivories was doing an Eagles tune when the man I'd been sitting beside evidenced his love of the song with a slightly intoxicated "Wa hoo!" as the first notes were played.

Midway through, a waiter picked up one of the extra microphones and began to sing different notes than the pianist was singing, creating what those in the "biz" call a harmony.

"Now that's pretty," said my new friend celebrating his 30th anniversary by visiting New York City for the first time, and a bit unsure, up to that moment, of how he felt about it and the group of men in heels singing along beside him.

And in silence I thought about what he said.

His "Now that's pretty" was the result of different notes being sung at the same time, in an uncanny case of a sum equaling more than the parts that make it up.

From some perspective, this man and the guys in heels beside him are part of a symphony.

From somewhere, something perceived this night and said, "Now that's pretty."

---★---

October 22, 2019

"I had the epiphany that laughter was light, and light was laughter, and that this was the secret of the universe."

—DONNA TARTT
THE GOLDFINCH

Tonight at *Hamilton*, a mom and her son came in very, very wet, and out of breath.

And laughing.

"What happened?" I asked.

"We got stuck in traffic and had to get out of the taxi and run like ten miles to get here on time!" the young man said with no little amount of exuberance.

"Maybe a half mile," his mom quietly told me, smiling at her soaked, shimmering son.

Then he said, "But I'm so excited I didn't even feel the rain! You can't feel rain when you're running to *Hamilton*!"

Another of *Hamilton's* super powers.

You can, though, sometimes feel the rain once *at Hamilton*, it turns out; during intermission Marie overheard a man telling the house manager that he'd been getting wet during the first act, and he couldn't figure out how. Thinking he was losing grasp of his senses, he asked his wife if she was experiencing the same thing. "Honey, my head is all wet. Is your head all wet?"

"What?"

"Is your head getting wet?"

"What are you talking about? Be quiet! Watch the show!"

Scolded, the man sat silently in his seat getting wetter by the moment, totally bumfuzzled as to how it was happening. Was someone fooling around with him, flicking water on him from behind? He twisted this way and that in his seat, trying to see who it could be, getting only blank, rather confused stares from his seat mates.

Eventually, he resigned himself to the fact he was becoming paranormally doused, and just let it happen, not wanting to miss any more of the show.

As it turned out, when the lights came up, he discovered that the more than hundred-year-old Richard Rodgers theater had sprung a leak in the roof, resulting in a drip drip that was falling only on him. "Ah ha!" he triumphantly said to his wife, and then to those around him. "Ah ha!!!"

Luckily, he told this story in high spirits and with a big smile.

Because that little boy who ran here in the rain with his mom is onto something.

There are some things the rain can't touch.

Some joys cannot be dampened.

October 24, 2019

I've recently lost 20 pounds, and was pretty excited when I realized, today, that my belly-donut has shrunk.

A few months ago, when I squished my belly together with both hands, the result resembled a giant donut. Today though, when I tried the same squish, I discovered a much more reasonably-sized donut.

So, I was feeling pretty good about my reasonably-sized belly donut tonight—when Chris Evans walked up to me.

Nothing makes your reasonably-sized belly donut feel less reasonable than when Captain America is standing in front of you.

I tried and tried, but no donut could be formed with his belly. (It was nice of him to let me give it a go, though).

And then, just in case I was still, at least, feeling okay about the progress I've made on my muscle tone, doing my ten pushups a day, the universe sent Dave Bautista (who plays Drax in the Marvel movies) to me about five minutes later.

So.

October 29, 2019

Tonight at *Hamilton*, a guy who was probably in his early eighties came up to buy sodas at intermission.

I often ask people how they are enjoying the show, because the answer is almost always an extremely positive one. It's pretty great to work someplace where the satisfaction rate is very nearly 100%, and I never tire of the "Oh my God!" reviews.

But I'll admit, when it's an older person, I sometimes worry. I don't mean to be ageist. It's just that I imagine this particular embodiment of storytelling might be so very different from what they have experienced in their eighty or so years.

So, when I asked this man tonight, "How's the show?" and he paused, unsmiling, I braced myself for one of the few lackluster reviews I've ever gotten.

"Well," he began, "I'll tell you something."

Here it comes, I thought.

"I can't understand a word they're saying. My hearing isn't good. My kids call me Old Man No Ears."

And when he laughed at that, I followed.

Then he said, "But . . . I love it! It's amazing. I can't hear it, but I know it's special. It's like when I was a kid and we had to read Romeo and Juliet and I had no idea what any of it meant. But I did know it was important somehow. I didn't get it, but I got that it was special. That's what this is like. My grandkids, though, they are over the moon right now. I may not be able to make out what these actors are saying, or follow what the heck Shakespeare was saying, but no one has to explain their faces to me!"

"Your drinks are on me," I said.

He didn't understand why, and it took some convincing, but eventually, perplexed and smiling now, he walked away, back to his grandkids who hadn't wanted to leave their seats.

Sometimes your brain gets things, and sometimes your heart does.

No ears required.

---- ★ ----

November 3, 2019

So, I've long had a crush on Anna Kendrick.

And I've long felt, if we could only meet, that she might find something about me appealing enough to at least want to get married.

As my pals know, I not long ago had a ridiculously vivid dream where I got to hang out with my soulmate for a while, and was told by some angel sort of dude that my soulmate and I aren't together "this time around," for whatever reason. So, I'm not looking for lifetimes worth of commitment here from Anna. Just the one.

As fate would have it, she is in a new show for HBO (called *Love Life*, just in case the universe hadn't hit me upside the head clearly enough already), and tomorrow, they are filming a scene in the *Hamilton* lobby.

And, as fate would also have it, they've asked me to be there for the day.

Of course, everyone involved believes they will be there to shoot an episode for a television show airing on HBO. I, though, know, and I suspect, Anna, deep in her heart, does too, that the whole thing is actually just a lovely ploy put on by the universe to place she and I together in the same room for one whole day.

Thanks, universe.

(I'll let you know how it goes)

---★---

November 5, 2019

After spending a day with Anna Kendrick, I can tell you I am well on my way to dreams coming true. While we didn't fall instantly in love, as I'd hoped, we did brush shoulders as we passed each other once.

"Oh, I'm sorry," she said.

"No, me, I'm sorry it's me, me sorry," very coolly responded I.

I realize "me sorry" is a bit more reminiscent of our imagined sense of cave people than English, but, Banana, being who she is, didn't mind it at all.

Here's what I can tell you so far about her:

1. When filming a scene, she does so in sweatpants and slippers, unless it's a wide shot.
2. She improvises easily and quickly, and those behind camera need to stifle laughs in order to not ruin the take.
3. She is every bit as lovely as you think she is.

> *P.S. The scene was about how bad our wine is at Hamilton. Just remember that while she is saying it, she's wearing sweatpants and slippers below the frame. You can't believe everything you see and hear on TV.*

—★—

December 13, 2019

"When I saw you I fell in love,
and you smiled
because you knew."

—ARRIGO BOITO
FALSTAFF

Hamilton is, essentially, a love story.

Sure, there's a lot more that goes on, like the founding of America and all the trouble that was, and whatnot, but in the end, what has thirteen hundred people crying every night—is a love story.

Like the founding of America, the love between Alexander and Eliza was not simple. There were ups and downs and in-betweens, and moments of acute pain. But no matter what happened in their marriage, no matter how grievously Eliza was hurt, her love for him endured. She spent the rest of her many years, in fact, after his untimely death, defending the man who'd so deeply wounded her.

Love, we find, even amidst the world and future-changing story of the creation of our democracy, is the story most worth telling. Taking place against a background that blazes, it is the connection between Eliza and Hamilton that shines brighter still, and is what has people reaching each night for their handkerchiefs.

Well, last night, I got a glimpse of why that is.

I sat in a four-seater on the train, and just before we pulled away, a woman sat down across from me.

And she was stunning.

I've ridden the train thousands of times, at this point, and never has this happened. I, reading my book about archeology, and she, this goddess, suddenly speaking to me, asking if I minded her sitting there.

"Is it okay?"

"Yes, of course, definitely, of course, for sure, yes," I calmly sputtered.

I feigned reading my book, while what I actually did was see her again in my mind. Was she truly as beautiful and smart and kind (somehow I just knew she

246

was smart and kind) as I'd seen her to be? I needed to be sure, so I quickly snuck another look as she stood up to remove her jacket and place her bag on the rack above our seats.

And, she was. She was take-your-breath-away beautiful, with eyes that betrayed her benevolent wisdom and intense intelligence.

While I continued the charade of "reading," she said, "Oh, I love that book!"

Was she talking to me? I wondered. *Was this created-in-a-lab human being speaking unsolicited to ME???*

She was. I looked up to see her smiling, and eked out a response.

Together we spoke, each passing moment my heart beating faster and better, too, it felt. Somehow, it was beating better than before. This person and I were connecting. We were clearly vibrating on some level unique to just the two of us, as she got my jokes before I made them, and I felt her laughter before I heard it. At one point, she removed her glasses to wipe tears from her eyes as we guffawed over a quip about mummies and ancient Egypt.

Wow.

This must be what all the fuss is about, I thought. *This is the feeling that has launched a million stories. This is what forced so much ink from Hamilton's pen. If all of the ridiculous effort of creating the universe, and the billions and trillions of years it took to unfold had been initiated simply to produce this one moment, this holy finding of each other, all of the ridiculous effort was worth it. The mystery of why the universe was made has been solved. It was for this. For us.*

And then her boyfriend got back from the bathroom and congratulated her on finding such a great seat.

So, you know . . . the universe remains a mystery.

---★---

December 14, 2019

"We know what we are, but not what we may be."
—WILLIAM SHAKESPEARE
HAMLET

I used to think I wanted to be famous.

After college, some of my friends actually became famous, and lived the lives we once dreamt about on winter nights over hot chocolate in cold, cramped New York City apartments. And, to be sure, a lot of what we imagined fame to be, turned out to be true for my friends. For instance, people lighting up simply at your walking into a room is something that happens, and of that aspect of notoriety, no one tires. The tendency to change how people feel for the better just by showing up, just by being there . . . well that's a real life super power. Of all the wonderful things that have happened to my uber talented friends who have found fame and fortune, this is the one and only that I envy of them—the ability to so easily make people feel better.

Tonight, though, a woman came up to me with her two young children. She said that she loves the *Hamilton* stories I write, and that she often shares them with her girls. And she and her girls beamed at me as she asked if she could take a photograph.

This occasionally happens, now. A person will come up and say, "I follow you on Facebook!" And I'll instantly begin to go over in my mind how my interaction with the person in front of this person who "knows" me went. *Was I friendly enough? Did I smile? Did I live up to the version of me people see in the stories I share?*

It's a tiny-minuscule-microscopic-quantum-sized version of the fame some friends have gained, but it still always makes me think.

Later, this sweet woman sent me a message that read, "Mike, the girls said, 'he's just as nice in person as his posts are!'"

But here's the thing; on a typical day, I'm not any nicer than the average person. In fact, lots of the people I know, like my mom and sisters and people I work with and *so* many others, are far more kind than I am. They are much better people than I. The only reason people read what I write is because I exploit a gift

248

my mom and dad gave me, which is the propensity to see what's good. But that doesn't make me any nicer than anyone else. The "fame" I've cultivated isn't me. It isn't real.

I just, because of my mom and dad, focus on peoples' capacity.

We almost never live up to what we are capable of. Most of the time, lots of us are petty and small and sort of, you know . . . gross. Because it ain't easy bein' a person. But every now and again, we transcend the things we usually do, and become the thing we really are.

Sometimes, we reach our capacity.

And those are the moments that touch me and I write about.

So, I want to use my tiny-minuscule-microscopic-quantum-sized "fame" to say to the wonderful young ladies I met last night, that it's an enormous honor to know that your mom sometimes shares the stories I write with you. And I'm so happy to know you thought I was "just as nice in person." But I'd like you to know also that it's not always easy to be nice, and that sometimes you won't be. You'll make mistakes and hurt people, and let yourselves down. You'll feel guilt and sadness and all sorts of awful, on the way of becoming. And you'll see a bunch of it on the news and in the world, too, as others go through the same struggles.

And it's all okay.

Because it's the capacity that you have to be amazing, to be compassionate, to love—it's the best of what is within you that *is* you.

You won't be it every day.

But every day it will be you, whether you know it or not.

That's what's real.

———————★—·———————

December 23, 2019

"Yes, Virginia, there is a Santa Claus.

There is a veil covering the unseen world which not the strongest man, nor even the united strength of all the strongest men that ever lived, could tear apart. Only faith, fancy, poetry, love, romance, can push aside that curtain and view and picture the supernal beauty and glory beyond.

Is it all real? Ah, Virginia, in all this world there is nothing else real and abiding."

—FRANCIS PHARCELLUS CHURCH

Tonight at intermission, I asked a young lady what she thought of the show.

"It's the best thing ever. Last Christmas, Santa gave us tickets, so I have been waiting forever for this. I've been waiting the whole year!" Then she asked, "Did you see him when he came to get them?"

I have a very complicated relationship with Santa. For many years longer than would be considered "normal," I defended the things my parents told me.

Other kids made a good bit of fun of me for it, too.

But convinced I remained. I simply couldn't fathom the idea that my mom and dad had misled me. It just wasn't something they would do.

And when I eventually realized some things, I was crushed. I really was. It turned my world upside down for a while there.

Of course, I knew why I was told what I was, and harbored nothing but great love for the people who told me, understanding the great love that led them to do it.

But, still, it stung.

"Did you see Santa when he came to get the tickets?"

"Well," I said. "I'm not sure. You know, Santa is magic, so he can be invisible. He might have come and I didn't see him because of his magic." To which she said, this five-year-old seer, "Well, this show is magic, and I saw that!"

What a roller coaster ride Santa and I have been on. Ups and downs in the extreme have had we.

My thanks to this little lady tonight, who reminded me that my mom and dad have never, not once, led me astray.

Magic, pals, is real.

And I know some places where you can find it.

December 27, 2019

Not long after *Hamilton* opened, the heart of one of our dear friends stopped as he stood in front of the theater. Someone came in and frantically told us that Thomas, one of the theater staff, was lying unconscious outside, his feet on the sidewalk and his head in the street. Marie, who loves Thomas, as we all do, immediately ran to get the defibrillator that we keep outside of my office. He was hooked up to it, and it said, "Shock needed," and we pressed the button and his body jumped and his heart began beating again.

A few days later, Marie and I went to see him in the hospital. He cried when we came in, then tried to say something. His throat was very sore from the tube that had been inserted, so he could barely speak above a whisper. He motioned for us to come closer and then closer, until our ears were right by his face.

"I saw you," he said with tears in his eyes.

"When?"

"When I was gone. I came out and went up, and I saw you there. I saw everyone. I came out."

Over the last few years, I've spent a lot of time researching "near death experiences." Many of the thousands upon thousands of cases leave no doubt in many minds, including mine, that what at least some of these people are experiencing is objectively real. There is simply too much evidence to put it all down to hallucinations and some trick of an oxygen-deprived brain.

This was very much on my mind today as my shaking hands fumbled to open the defibrillator and remove the contacts from their pouches.

A man had come downstairs to the lobby as *Hamilton* pumped around us, and said, "My father is unresponsive."

By the time I got upstairs with the gear, our two security people had pulled the man in his chair from the box he was in.

Then, we closed the curtain. The pulsing life of *Hamilton* was separated by a mere piece of cloth from the commencement of a gargantuan struggle. Not two feet from us, heads bobbed to the music, completely unaware that behind them a man lay on the floor, releasing from life.

After cutting off his shirt, the contacts were placed on his chest. The machine must have detected a faint heartbeat, because it said to commence CPR, rather than administering the charge.

"Push harder," the computer voice calmly advised.

I sat helplessly as Ed and Jimmy, our security people, took turns furiously pushing on this man's chest while his son stood over our shoulders.

"Push harder," it repeated. Ed, already giving all he had, sweat dripping from his brow, found more strength, and pushed harder. "Okay take a break, take a break," Jimmy insisted, as he took over the herculean effort.

Eventually, the ambulance arrived, and the large man was finally carried by ten firefighters down the narrow staircase that leads to the boxes. They placed him in the ambulance, and it drove away as we all looked on, shaken and in silence.

When we first got to the man, he was still in his seat.

He hadn't made any commotion whatsoever, it seemed. I think his son happened to notice that his dad's eyes had closed, then tried to wake him, but couldn't.

He just sort of, I think, slipped out.

As these complete strangers, in a dark, cramped corner of the theater, fought and fought to bring him back, I wondered where the man was. I wondered if he, like Thomas, had "come out," and was witnessing the ferocious effort to save him from above.

And I suddenly felt this love . . . for people.

I felt this general, all-encompassing love.

Being a person is just so freaking hard.

We focus a lot on the things we do wrong. The news streams twenty-four hours a day of the wrong.

But confronted with this life and death situation today, face to face with it, all I could feel was love for every single person there.

Struggling together, to be human.

---★---

January 29, 2020

"But the effect of her being on those around her was incalculably diffusive: for the growing good of the world is partly dependent on unhistoric acts; and that things are not so ill with you and me as they might have been, is half owing to the number who lived faithfully a hidden life, and rest in unvisited tombs."

—GEORGE ELIOT
MIDDLEMARCH

On my way from Grand Central to the theater, and then back after the show, every day I pass people sitting or sleeping or living on the sidewalk asking for "Any help I can spare." I keep singles in my pocket for these walks, specifically to give someone who asks. I hand them the dollar and try to catch their eye. There is such hustle and bustle blurring the struggle in Manhattan, that individual interactions are often lost amongst the sea of activity big cities provide. I can only hope a person knows I see them, wishing I could truly help, and not just pass a dollar bill. Usually, though, after they ask a God they somehow still believe in to bless me, and I thank them for that wish, our exchange is over. Tonight, though, someone saw me.

After the show, I'd gone a few blocks uptown to celebrate the birthday of a coworker, and having so enjoyed the company of my pals, I lost track of time.

At 1:38am I realized I needed to immediately catch a cab if there was any chance of getting on the 1:47am train from Grand Central, which was the last train home to Connecticut.

Well, by less than five-seconds, I missed it. As my fingers helplessly grasped at them, the doors shut closed.

I waited inside the warm station until a police officer not so patiently "asked" me to leave. So, back outside I went, into the cold.

I sat on the sidewalk and pulled up Hotel Tonight on my phone. This is an app that gets you good deals on last minute rooms. However, my phone is older and a little glitchy, and I couldn't get it to understand that I wanted a room for right now, for tonight, and not the "today" the app understood, which was, for me, tomorrow. I eventually gave up on the app and thought, *Well, it's 2:30. The next train to Connecticut leaves at 5:49. I can wait 3 hours.*

I curled up in a corner, pulled the hood of my hoodie as far over my ears as it would go, and tried to find a comfortable position. Which I eventually sort of found.

"Hey man. Hey . . . hey man."

I had dozed off, and was awoken by a person gently saying, "Hey man."

When I'd been fully roused from my sidewalk slumber, he said, "I've got some space here, if you want to use it."

The space he had was a bit of cardboard attached to the unit he'd set up.

"Oh, thank you!" I said. "It's okay—I'm just waiting a couple of hours for a train."

"Gotcha," he said. "Well, if you change your mind, this spot here," as he gestured toward a portion of his makeshift sleeping space, "is for you."

And as this man who has "nothing" smiled while offering some of his "nothing" to me, I realized why it takes years of meditation and solitary climbing of mountains and sitting cross-legged by streams to begin to conceive words like "having" and "nothing."

His nothing is the most I've ever been given.

February 6, 2020

Tonight at *Hamilton*, two young girls, maybe ten, came up to the bar.

Here from Pennsylvania on a school trip, they were absolutely ecstatic to be at *Hamilton*, and said as much to Marie (who, being a kid in an adult body, connects quite well with innocent, pure joy, such as is to be found in dogs and children).

After showing Marie the special stuffed animal these best friends had brought with them in a backpack all the way to New York, so that Milky, the cotton-filled cow, could also enjoy *Hamilton*, they bounced away into the theater.

At intermission, they came back, and this time ended up in my line. One ordered a Sprite and the other a Ginger Ale. As I began to pour the first, they asked how much a soda was. "They're eight dollars," I said, and anxiety flashed across their faces.

Between them, I soon understood, they had only ten dollars—five each—enough to get just one soda.

And that's when the great battle began.

For some time, as the line quickly gathered in large numbers behind them, they debated.

In one of the best interactions I've ever witnessed, the girl who wanted the Sprite tried to convince her friend a Ginger Ale was, now that she really thought about it, the better idea, while the girl who had asked for the Ginger Ale suddenly realized Sprite was the superior beverage.

As the "fight" went on, I poured both drinks.

When they finally looked back at me, flush with worry that their friend was not going to get what she really wanted, I slid a Sprite and a Ginger Ale over the bar.

It took quite some time to get them to understand that I wasn't charging for the drinks.

And when they finally did understand, the appreciation reached a level that makes me weepy right now, as I type.

So, as the world around us sends signals of apparent great discord and unrest and sadness into our brains, know that tonight, two young girls refused to order the thing they wanted, preferring instead, the happiness of her pal.

And that desire is more prevalent than we think.

———————————★———————————

February 20, 2020

"What is the meaning of life? That was all- a simple question; one that tended to close in on one with years, the great revelation had never come. The great revelation perhaps never did come. Instead, there were little daily miracles, illuminations, matches struck unexpectedly in the dark; here was one."

—Virginia Woolf
To the Lighthouse

There's a curious feature of human memory.

As time passes, we tend to theatricalize and poeticize events we've experienced. Rather than recalling in granular detail everything that's occurred, some unplumbed process records not just the sights and sounds and other senses, but also the emotions we've had, and adjusts memories, sometimes, based on them. Which makes memory a very tricky thing. It's a shifting, alterable "truth," that recent science shows changes each time we access it—the very act of bringing up a past event, we now believe, alters the way that event is relived in our minds.

I think history might be similarly subject to some mechanism that grinds down rough edges, leaving polish behind. America, for instance, has an actual history, and also the one many "remember." The one most recall is painted in glorious colors, and probably with a copiously inspirational soundtrack running underneath. It's Stars and Stripes and heroics and beautiful bravery, the likes of which it might seem difficult to currently reach. And that's because those levels of beauty are typically only attained with years. It takes a great passage of time and many retellings for events to be compressed to peaks and valleys. Perhaps the accumulated weight of years acts on our sense of the past the way pressure does on carbon deep within the earth, resulting, eventually, in diamonds.

Watching the Democratic debate tonight, what might therefore stand out is the ugliness.

Because the making of a country, in real time, is hard, dirty work. In the moment, no matter how noble the cause within a heart, things are said and done that do not reflect that nobility.

This has always been the case. To make the gem that we think of with such splendor as "America," much toil and pain and downright terribleness happened.

The truth is not always the poetry time makes it. But it doesn't mean the poetry isn't there. The noble causes within those hearts is the poetry. The desire for better is the poetry.

The way we get there, often, is not.

As the debate went on in the background, being televised from the phone hidden on my register, I spoke with a mom who came up to the bar. Her young son, she told me, had a brain tumor, and for the long while he was in the hospital, the soundtrack of *Hamilton* is what kept his spirits up. Something about the music brought him joy and gave him hope.

And, thank all that is good, the surgery and recovery went well.

So tonight, her little boy got to sit in the orchestra, feet away from people singing the music that helped to keep him going. And as she told me the story, and described his face as the show began (which she then looked at for the entire first act, rather than the stage), I couldn't help but be unable, for a moment, to respond.

I pressed the button that turned off the screen of my phone.

Because every now and again, time isn't necessary to make poetry. Sometimes, poetry happens right there in front of you.

March 1, 2020

The little man in this photo is special.

His mom and I grew up in the same town, and he doesn't know it, and neither does she, but they are heroes of mine.

See, it can be so hard, and so hair-raising, being a person. And in his very young life, he and his family have faced the most trying and frightening things life can muster. Things, you'd imagine, that make smiles impossible.

And they don't smile.

They radiate. They shoot sunbeams out of their faces.

Somehow, having braved medical trials no one should, they've come out sun-beaming.

Tonight, after the show, we went up on stage, and Patrick began to perform the first number, "Alexander Hamilton."

Well, (with my apologies, Lin) in my five years of listening daily to the show, it's easily the best rendition of the song I've yet heard.

Not long ago, Patrick decided he wanted to paint rocks to spread his joy around.

Today, I, and the entire *Hamilton* cast, got our own joy rocks.

And, man, do they freakin' work!

Remember this, pals; you aren't the stuff life throws at you.

You are the rocks you paint afterwards.

--- ★ ---

March 4, 2020

*"At some point in life the world's beauty becomes enough. You don't
need to photograph, paint, or even remember it. It is enough."*
—Toni Morrison
Tar Baby

It occurs to me that I've now spent as much time working at *Hamilton* as I did in college. When I was in college, five years felt like such a significant amount of time. And now, five years is but a drop in the bucket of years I've lived since. If you were to ask me which of the five-year periods (sometimes college takes five years, friends) had the greatest impact on my life, which stretch was more formative, I'd not be able to answer.

As I sit in this coffee shop between shows on a rainy Wednesday afternoon, watching a group of blazing leaves hanging stubbornly on from the fall, being lifted from the sidewalk by a supportive spiraling wind, an invisible eddy urging them in multicolored swirls on to what's next, I'm thinking about all of the things that have happened during my time on the tree of *Hamilton*.

I've had experiences that, were I to be able to travel back in time and tell my fifteen-year-old self about, he would, once again, like in first grade, pee his pants. He would not believe that such wonderful things are in his future. He'd not believe the "future him" (even though he'd just stepped out of a time machine, which you'd think would give sufficient weight to what "future him" had to say) when "future him" tells "past him" that he'll twice meet maybe the best president ever, a president that "past him" doesn't even know he needs yet. Fifteen-year-old him, struggling there in early high school to fit in, to just find a place in it all that doesn't hurt too much, trying to believe Bruce Springsteen's words that "Better days are shining through," will never be convinced by "future him," no matter how spectacularly the time machine whirs there in all its futuristic glory, when he tells him that, one day, not only will he meet The Boss, but that he'll ask him to write a song, an anti-anthem about a president that will come after the one he doesn't yet know he needs, and is far more frightening than any president his fifteen-year-old mind can conjure or believe is possible, and that that song will eventually be released by Bruce

260

(I'm not certain that I can take *complete* credit for it, as it had already been penned when I asked him, but, you know, we're dealing with time travel here, so things get weird). "Past me" would be absolutely stunned to learn that meeting Springsteen would just be the beginning of the meetings he will have, all of the hands of the extraordinary people that "then me" is reading about in books and watching on TV and seeing on the thirty-foot screen at the movie theater, he will get to shake.

"Past me" will doubt "future me" entirely when I tell him that he will thank Mark Ruffalo ("Who?" he will ask. "Just listen, dude" I will say) for his activism and Katy Perry for her kindness.

He will tell CC Sabathia he was taller and nicer than he thought he'd be, and with that learn what his laugh sounds like.

He will get to hang out with Chris Rock and Ed Norton and Ethan Hawk and Sandra Bullock and, of course, meet his girlfriend, Banana, and (still) future wife, Jessica Biel, and see up close the prince of some country (which is a fake thing I can't believe we still have) and a real prince named Prince (right now, for you, but he won't be named that always . . . someday he will be The Artist Formerly Known as Prince, and then just a symbol for a while, but, by the time you meet him, I think he is back to Prince again . . . the future isn't always simple, young lad), and Beyoncé (who for you right now is a member of a little-known group in Houston. You'll come to know her in a few years as Beyoncé Knowles of Destiny's Child, but when you see her at *Hamilton* she will have become The Queen—with much more influence than the Queen you know now, and can't believe is still a real thing).

He will meet the entire San Antonio Spurs and US Olympics Gymnastic teams, and tell them how nice it is to have athletes in the house that are of a similar level of physical ability as him—at which, oddly, they all, every single one, will laugh (sorry to break it to you this way kid, but you don't end up starting for the Red Sox—that growth spurt you're waiting on, it ends up going a little more in the horizontal direction than you're hoping for . . . but, listen, just go down the hall and step into that theater you're afraid of. The scary leaps you take are going to be when the best stuff happens).

He'll find out that Mark Cuban and Jerry Jones and Oprah Winfrey, though some of the wealthiest people on the planet, are, when it comes down to it, no different from you and me. They will live and laugh and love, and one day, not be here. They struggle. And no amount of money solves the big things like lone-liness and fear.

And he will meet hundreds of others who everyone on the planet knows. The most famous human beings that have ever been. People that some folks dream of meeting.

But of all "past me" hears "future me" say about all that neat stuff, what will **SURPRISE** him most is to learn that meeting these people will not come close to being the best thing that happens to him—that, in fact, those experiences pale in comparison to the uncontrollable laugh he'll have that continues to bubble up for hours when Marie (a person he doesn't yet know, but who will eventually make it impossible for him to recall what the world was like before her) says this funny thing one arbitrary day. They don't compare to the encouragement Andy, his future pal and co-worker, gives him when he shares the first clip of a project he's working on about life-after-death ("Wait, go back . . . what?" "past me" will ask. "That's another story," I'll say, "But man, you are going to learn that the universe is way crazier than Mr. Vance tells you it is later today in period 7 physics!), and how supportive Andy is when he tells him about writing this book ("I write a book?" he will interrupt. "You do," I'll say. "Do you hear that, Mr. Mikulack?" he will shout). These wonderful *Hamilton* experiences will match, in no way, the joy he will feel when his littlest sister tells him she's discovered the love of her life, and asks him to be the reverend at her wedding ("I become a revered?!?" he'll spit out with now complete disbelief. "Yes, but that's a surpris-ingly easy thing to do in the future. You don't even need to take a quiz—after a small payment over the internet, boom, you're ordained."

"Internet . . . ?"

"We don't have time right now—you're gonna love it, though. Orders of mag-nitude easier than the hours upon hours upon painful hours digging through microfiche you'll be doing for Mrs. Carleton's history project next year").

Never, in a million years, would he trade the cup of coffee he will have with our mom one early morning, as we watch the birds from her porch and talk about life, or the lotteries he won when his sisters, Jen and Stefanie, became his siblings, for the experiences he will have with *Hamilton*.

Here, then, is the best news "future me" has to share with "past me;" the most powerful thing that *Hamilton* will give you, is what it won't.

What makes life *life*, what makes it the wonder that it is, and worth all the great trouble, is not glitz and glamour and bright lights and fame and fortune. True wealth is not related to the coinage it is so often associated with. The real treasure is the connections you make. It's the people you choose to go along for the ride with on this spectacular odyssey.

The best things, the only ones that really matter, truly, can only be found in those beside you.

Which is why meeting Barack Obama and watching *Hamilton* unfold in all of its glory won't be the coolest thing that ever happens to you; standing beside Marie and Andy when it happens, is.

FINALE

"October knew, of course, that the action of turning a page, of ending a chapter or of shutting a book, did not end a tale. Having admitted that, he would also avow that happy endings were never difficult to find: "It is simply a matter," he explained to April, "of finding a sunny place in a garden, where the light is golden and the grass is soft; somewhere to rest, to stop reading, and to be content."

—NEIL GAIMAN
SEASON OF MISTS

Today is June 11th, 2020. It has been three months since Broadway closed down due to the COVID-19 pandemic. Three months since the world stopped, and even "The City That Never Sleeps" ground to a halt. Three months since so much we take for granted, so suddenly wasn't.

When I was little, and home sick from school, the day took on a special feeling. While the rest of the world on its wobbly way went, there laid I on the couch, so warmly tucked in by my mom. The other kids, the classmates my anxieties made certain I barely knew, picked up where they'd left off the day before, learning this and that, and also, sometimes, being mean to each other.

The rare days I stayed home "sick" were something of a respite. A chance to be with just my mom, surrounded only by love.

A reset, in some way.

I got recharged on those days. And not just physically. Being at home with just my mom and *The Price is Right,* while the earth spun ahead without us, allowed my brain to get quiet. And when the brain gets quiet, it's amazing what you can hear.

We're born with this voice that speaks to us. By a certain age, we almost always forget it's there. The noise of living so easily drowns it out, and with such a thoroughness that we eventually no longer recall it even existed.

It did, though.

The voice used to remind us, in its quiet and gentle way, what we want out of life. Why we came here. Why we chose, in the first place, to do this very crazy and terrifying thing.

This human thing.

It got hard to hear the voice very early on. The moment I was made fun of for my hairstyle, the result of the home-cut my dad would do to save money, the voice got overshadowed by another. This new voice wanted to protect me. This voice realized the world isn't a safe place, and quickly built barriers to defend against it.

This voice came from my brain. That other voice, the quiet one, the one that loved my family and the sky at night and the way the shell my dad threw skipped an impossible number of times over the water, and rainbows and space shuttle launches and the beautiful sound my mom made with just her voice as she sang us to sleep, and the smell of the grass on the baseball field, and everything that was amazing about being a person came from somewhere else, I sensed. I didn't know from where, but it definitely wasn't the same place that worried about what the kids at school would say about my Kmart clothes.

On those sick days, I could hear it again. More so than my body, it was my spirit that got healed on those days.

Because we've all got cracks in the fortresses where the truth can sink in and bubble up. There are seams, always seams—the armor the brain builds is not without pores, impregnable though it looks when we move so fast. So quickly do we go on an average day from thought to thought, keeping brains busy with what we mistake for importance, that the joints get blurred and lost in the whole, like a polychromatic top merging into one shade when spun. But you aren't the smudged perception that most often meets eyes. You aren't the spinning shield you've come to think of as you. You are the light that lives beneath the artifice, the protective construct, you are the ray that sometimes escapes when the spinning seams have slowed, you are the voice you hear from long ago that wondered how boats can float and planes can fly and the moon follows wherever you go.

And like a great wind athwart our incessant, obscuring motion, Mother Nature has said, to the whole world, "Slow down."

The whole world is on a sick day now.

And it's distressing and unprecedented and, for some, a matter of life and death. For some, it will be the way this life is exited.

This precious life.

Which is always, 100% of the time, exited.

But, there is also possibility. On some deep, perhaps even subconscious level, we're being shown in stark relief how connected we are. How much we need each other. How wonderful it is to hug. When was the last time you noticed the joy in shaking hands?

The sky over China is blue, and the water in Venice is clear.

We've slowed down so much that the earth has mended in some visible, if temporary, ways.

It's my deep hope that this world sick day will clear up some of the pollution in our brains, too, as the fissures grow more wide and the light gets in.

Maybe things will slow and quiet enough to hear the voice. And be reminded by it why we wanted to come in the first place, and how special a thing it is to be alive. And how much we need each other to do it.

I think often of the first night back at the theater, and what it will be like after this time apart, when Mama Earth sent us to our rooms to think about things. I imagine the joy we are going to feel when the curtain once again rises, and the stage springs to life after so long a dormancy. How amazing a thing it will be to sit again, together, while not taking that togetherness for granted, and watch a show. Because if there is anything this time out has reminded us, it is how there is something important about being in the same space. And it's not just a feeling we have . . . science has detected it, too.

In 2017, researchers from University College London observed audience members attending a performance of *Dreamgirls* in the West End. They hooked people up to equipment that monitored their heart rates and electrodermal activity—and what they found astounded them: the hearts of these strangers, sitting together experiencing the show, began to beat in sync. Something about the performance caused a coherence in their rhythms. At intermission, the effect dissipated, and resumed once again in the second act. The researchers have no idea why. Science can't explain it, as of yet. But we can. You and I, we know something science so far doesn't, and that this slowdown is making clear: we are connected in ways the eyes can't see, and our scientific instruments aren't yet sensitive enough to fully detect. And theater is one of the things that lights up those pathways between us, that strengthens, for a time, that bond, and causes the usually invisible strings tying us together to turn on.

So, I have been envisioning over and over again that first night back. When thirteen hundred strangers, after so long apart, will cry and laugh and learn together, and be strangers no more. We'll sit there together, hearts beating in time, and something deep in the universe will shift, I like to imagine. As the experience of *Hamilton* bursts wide our seams, and we flow with gratitude for this hallowed event whose precious nature we'd lost some sight of, and those in the vicinity slip out from beneath the thoughts of who they are, and the illusion of separation from all the other armors they see, and connect with all the other slips, connect so thoroughly that our hearts become synchronized . . . well, just imagine it.

Somehow, live theater does that. Even some baffled scientists in London say so.

I don't know what it might mean. But I do sense it must be important. And once Mother Nature allows us to spin again, perhaps it will be more slowly, so that it won't take a night at the theater with electrodermal monitors to realize we are one.

ENCORE

In 2015, when *Hamilton's* Broadway run was still in its infancy, and the vast majority of the original cast were still in the show, large trailer trucks pulled up in front of the theater.

Knowing full well, even then, the unmatched, once-in-a-lifetime nature of what they had on their hands, the producers early on decided to film the stage production for posterity. And as a large production company began to unload equipment, it became clear this would not be a few cameras set up statically at the back of the theater.

We usually don't know something is seminal when it happens, but with *Hamilton*, they did, making the endeavor to record it of the upmost importance. Any measures necessary would be taken to chronicle it in the fullest way possible. Live theater is its own medium, though, and no matter how much you do, it's impossible for the experience to translate completely—but they were going to try. Cameras were set up at multiple positions, some hanging from cranes and others strapped to people. Over the course of three days and two live performances, the show was documented from every angle, including Steadicam close-ups from near enough to capture the facial nuances audiences often aren't able to entirely perceive from their seats.

The word "on the street" was that the filming was a monumental success, and clamors for its release started early. Eventually, a plan had been put in place to theatrically premiere the film in late 2021. However, the circumstances of 2020 came along, and you know . . . ouch. Wanting to give people a blast of love and even a modicum of relief, it was decided the debut was to be pushed up to July 3rd of this harrowing year, streamed digitally to the safety of peoples' homes.

As I pressed play, I noticed an anxiety rise within me. Would this live up to my memories? Would the family and friends I've been haranguing with stories of *Hamilton's* magic see what I saw? Was it really what I thought it was? Well, by the time the ensemble sang the word "forgiveness," and Lin drew a quick breath at the touch of Eliza's hand, I was sobbing alone in my living room.

I'd been right. Magic.

A friend and I were watching the show separately but at the same time, sharing our reactions along the way. At one point, I sent her a photo of my teary countenance, and she sent back emojis denoting care and love. And though watching *Hamilton* on my television screen was heart-stirring and joyous, still . . . something was missing. Emojis can be nice, but nothing beats a real face connected to a real heart beating beside you. And it got me thinking about what *Hamilton* is like, there in that room, and how profoundly I miss it.

I'll often walk into the theater during the last song, not to watch the show, but the audience.

Ever since that glorious evening when Marie and I and just a few others got to see *Hamilton,* in a big, empty venue, using all of the extra oxygen in the gaping Richard Rodgers Theatre to quench our expanding emotions, leaving us, by the end, big, blubbering blobs, I've reveled in the nightly opportunity to witness others experience it for the first time.

To hear the sniffles, to see the tears glistening on so many faces, and often, the grabbing of a seat-mate's hand, suddenly reminded of how thankful they are for the love of the person beside them—to see so many people, so many strangers, sitting together, every night, in a theater, responding this way to a play, well . . . there's magic in that.

Because, about 15 million years ago (depending on who you trust for that sort of information), a human being woke up and found herself aware. She looked out at the vast expanse of ocean, and then up to the endless sky. And she was afraid. Quickly she scrambled, searching for an answer. Surely, instructions had been left. Somewhere, she was sure, a manual must be, describing what this was. What the meaning of it was. And, of course, the meaning of her. What was she? And where did she come from? And why, goodness why, was she here? But there was

no manual. No guide showed up to point the way, and no letter was found saying, "So, here's the deal . . ." As it turned out, the only tools she'd have on this
quest to understand, were her mind, and her heart. And as day turned to night,
millions of lights began to show themselves. She had no idea what they were. But
as more and more appeared, the depth of the sky increased, and she realized how
small she was. The weight of the towering night could have been crushing. She
didn't have to bear it alone, though. There were others. So many others, she'd
discover. But they were all unique. All had their own ideas about what should be
done. All of them stuffed full, by whatever does the stuffing, with desires and
proclivities and behaviors so diverse they matched the number of sky twinkles.
And somehow, without any directions, and their multitude of wants and needs
and greeds and fears, they needed to work out, together, how to be.

The chances they'd make it were stupendously small.

If you'd granted a certain form of life awareness, but only enough to understand how little it understands, and put it in the conditions described, you
wouldn't expect it to survive. Especially if you'd given no hints—no instructions
about what life is for, or what to do with it. And most especially if you *did* give
some hints, but somehow in translation, wires got crossed and messages confused
and some thought the hints meant one thing, and some something different, and
others something else altogether.

If, 15 million years later, you looked down, or up or over or wherever, and
found anything but a barren wasteland, with the odds, as they were, so thoroughly stacked against them, you'd surely be stunned.

But if you were to find them not only still there, but sitting together in a
theater . . .

Rare, indeed, life seems to be. More exceptional still, must be a species that
expresses its awareness like this; through music and movement and pretending. If
there is some all-powerful being that created the universe, then set it all on its way
to see where it'd go, this being must not only be interested in us, but positively
beguiled; because not even an omniscience could have imagined that profound
existential questions, such as the ones we woke up with all those years ago, amidst
the impossible circumstances in which we asked them, would be answered not
with utter and complete despair, but on the contrary, with singing and dancing.

"People, here's what we know; the universe seems to be pretty big, and possibly
infinite, whatever that means. We don't have any idea what it all portends, if

anything, or where it's going, if anywhere, or why. Basically, we have absolutely no understanding of . . . anything at all. So, here's what we'll do: let's come up with stories, and some catchy songs, and combine them with fantastic accompanying choreography. Then we'll sit in the dark, and look towards the light. And in it, those stories will be told. And, together, we'll cry, and laugh, and love. And when we need to, hold hands."

Looking in on the end of *Hamilton*, and seeing all of the above, who or whatever put this thing into motion, if it has thoughts, could form only one:

"How amazing."

WHO KNOWS?

On the night that Donald Trump was elected, the swing of the pendulum nearly knocked me out. From my perspective, we'd gone from a poet, from Plato's predicted "philosopher king," to a man stuck deeply in Plato's cave.

I spent the next days in a daze, as my mom and sister, and many other women, in particular, in my life, literally wept. The election of this person was a psychological trauma to them, and we desperately struggled to recover from the shock and fear.

It was a dark time for so many.

There is no way, though, that I could have prophesied the personal experiences this event would precipitate. There is no way I could have known, for instance, that the universe would conspire to put me in a position where I'd meet Mike Pence, and get to tell him, face to very close face, that I believe, "Love is love is love is love is love is love is love is love."

Most importantly, I did not imagine that my writing about that experience would bring into my life so many beautiful people.

That it would bring into my life . . . you.

There is a Taoist story that goes something like this:

A Chinese farmer gets a horse, which soon runs away. A neighbor comes over and says, "I'm so sorry to hear about your horse!"

The farmer replies, "Who knows what's good or bad?"

The next day, the horse returns. With friends. The farmer now has ten horses.

The same neighbor comes over to congratulate his friend on his good fortune.

But again the farmer responds, "Who knows what's good or bad?"

The following week, the man's son is attempting to tame one of the horses, when he is thrown from her back and breaks his leg.

"I'm sorry about your son," says the neighbor, which elicits the very same answer, "Who knows?"

Finally, the next day, the army comes to the town to enlist all of the able-bodied young men, who will fight a battle in which almost all will perish. Because of the broken leg, the man's son is not among them.

You get the point.

On the night of November 8th, 2016, I felt lower than I had in a long time. But then that election brought all of you into my life.

This book, friends, is for my mom, and it's for you, the virtual connections I've met over these difficult days that have kept me not only aloft, but *knowing* that we will be okay . . . that the pendulum will, indeed, swing back.

The basic current of humanity's evolution is clearly going in one direction, if we can see it from a distant enough perspective.

And that direction is love.

No doubt about it, pals.

LIKE A HANDPRINT
ON MY HEART

Here is a picture of the first and best thing to ever happen to me:

My mom worked ridiculously hard to send me to college. She thought the classes I took there would plant the seeds of the tree I'd eventually climb to reach happiness. What she didn't know, though, was that no college course could ever come close to teaching me what I actually needed to learn to find that particular thing.

The only class I really needed began to take shape on February 17th, 1952. That is the day (not so long ago, she'll have you know) that Elizabeth Bonaldo, my mom, was born. It's the anniversary of a day when an uncountable number of events were set into motion. Most of these events one might see as "small" in nature. Events like smiles and hugs and late-night words of advice.

In one "small" moment she handed a dollar to a man who seemed to be living on the streets. But it wasn't really a dollar. It was love disguised as a dollar. As she handed it over, she gently touched his shoulder and waited for him to look up. She gazed into his face and silently said, with only her eyes, "I see you. You are a human being. Nothing separates me from you but happenstance. I am no better or worse. With all of my heart, stranger, I wish I could lighten your unfair load."

Her children got to witness that. An event that took only seconds, which I doubt she even remembers. How could she, being mixed, as it is, with so many other similar seconds?

But, since her kids were there, that moment set into motion a million more "small" events. So you see, when you add it all up . . . you simply can't. The ripples that started with her birth, not so long ago, she'll have you know, are infinite. She is not aware of the power of her smile and hugs and love.

Every year at Thanksgiving, she tries to make a toast. We'll all be gathered around her table, talking in our loud Italian way, and she'll pick up a glass and start clinking it with a fork. We notice and get quiet; we know what's coming, and start to smile as we look towards the woman who brought us all together. She lifts the glass to us, and her lips begin to tremble. She opens her mouth to speak, but before a syllable is uttered, she starts to cry. Overcome with the emotion of being there with her family, that's where the toast ends.

This is an annual occurrence. Every year she tries, and every year she can't quite get the words out. It's something we gently tease her about—as soon as she picks up the glass, her grandchildren wonder aloud if this will be the year that something is said.

Despite the teasing, though, we know we are witnessing something profound.

I have long been aware that tears are special. They are an expression of God or the universe or love or who or whatever makes this thing spin. When we are vulnerable enough to cry, we are touching something more true than we typically tap into in our everyday lives. For a few moments, we let the armor fall away. The fortress we have constructed around ourselves to get through this battle, this life, crumbles, just for a time. And ever so briefly, we are who we are—which is who we were before so much life happened to us. We touch God or the universe or love or who or whatever makes this thing spin, and it fills us up.

And the excess leaks from our eyes.

So, though we make gentle fun, we know what those tears mean. So stuffed full of God or the universe or love is my mom, that she leaks all the time.

And she never cries more so than when she reads a comment someone has made to a story I've shared. See, my mom always thought I was meant to be a writer.

"You *need* to write!" She'd constantly declare, no matter the middling letter grade my middle school essay on *To Kill A Mockingbird* received. And I'd always respond, "Mom, you like my writing because you're my mom! You said the same thing when I brought home my artwork in second grade—which I recently found in the attic. And either A) you are a terrible critic, or B) you lied to me when you extolled my talent." She continued to insist, though, which is why you're now reading this.

She's always been my biggest fan. And if you knew her, you'd be hers.

And now if I write something, and she finds it has somehow positively affected someone, she is overcome with emotion. If she discovers it helped someone feel better, even just a little, well, the spigot opens. The idea that any of her children may have been a part of lifting someone's spirit makes her brim with joy. But what she doesn't realize is this: if there is any usefulness in us, she put it there. If we are prone to noticing the good in people, it's because she taught us how to look. If we sit and wonder at the magnificence of the stars, and try to see how big it all is, and how precious all of us are, it is because she pointed at the sky. If we treat all people—no matter the amount of money they have or don't, or the color of their skin, or the faith they have chosen, or the people they love—with the same respect, it is because my mom directed our attention not to what makes us different, but to what makes us alive.

So, Mom, you see, any good we happen to do, you do. If someone's spirit has been lifted by something I've written, you lifted it. Because *you* wrote it.

So when I said earlier that, "This book is for my mom," I wasn't quite accurate.

The book isn't *for* you;

It's *your* book.

Thanks for letting me put my name on it.

—"So much of me is made of what I learned from you."

Made in the USA
Middletown, DE
13 December 2020